2007
9X 4 10 8/11

PUNCHING IN

PUNCHING IN

The Unauthorized Adventures

of a Front-Line Employee

ALEX FRANKEL

Collins
An Imprint of HarperCollinsPublishers

HarperCollins books may be purchased for educational, business, or sales promotional use. For information, please write: Special Markets Department, HarperCollins Publishers, 10 East 53rd Street, New York, NY 10022.

FIRST EDITION

Designed by Joseph Rutt

Library of Congress Cataloging-in-Publication Data is available upon request.
ISBN: 978-0-06-084966-5
ISBN-10: 0-06-084966-5

07 08 09 10 11   OV/RRD   10 9 8 7 6 5 4 3 2

For Satoko

If, at my death, my executors, or more properly my creditors, find any precious MSS. in my desk, then here I prospectively ascribe all the honor and the glory to whaling; for a whale-ship was my Yale College and my Harvard.

—Herman Melville, *Moby-Dick*

CONTENTS

	Author's Note	xi
INTRODUCTION	Becoming One of Them	1
ONE	The Other Army	11
TWO	One Great Employee	51
THREE	Two Truths and One Lie	79
FOUR	Into the Fold	119
FIVE	Get Big, Stay Small	149
SIX	In the Red Zone	187
CONCLUSION	Self-Selection	201
	Endnotes	209
	Acknowledgments	213
	Index	215

AUTHOR'S NOTE

In the pages that follow, I have made up names for all of the workers I met during the course of reporting this book. I did this to preserve their anonymity and shield their true identities; if I were in their shoes, I would have expected similar treatment. Providing pseudonyms and rendering the people I met as characters also seemed to fit well with the way in which workers are all asked to play parts in what I came to see as a form of modern corporate theater.

The seminal narrative of the business world is the case study—a focused examination of an issue faced by a business. At their best, these corporate tales depict the commercial foundation that under-girds our contemporary society in its most vivid, Technicolor glory. For a few summers in high school, I worked at Stanford's business school collating and assembling these documents for executive courses taught each July. The more interesting cases read like Audubon field guides to capitalist human society. I spent more than a few warm summer nights reading about subjects that ranged from Renault's introduction of its front-drive subcompact Le Car into North America to Sony's launch of the original stereophonic blue-and-silver Walkman. Though some in my shoes might have been inspired to lead a company and shape the case studies of the future, I grew interested in living inside one. This book is my own immersive take on the case study.

PUNCHING IN

BECOMING ONE OF THEM

I was in the building at 8:20 when the center supervisor called a group meeting of the drivers. It was the same meeting every day, but I hadn't paid attention to what exactly transpired. The supervisor was named Pedro and he had a chiseled jaw, slicked his black hair straight back, and wore what looked like designer-frame eyeglasses. He stood about 6 foot 5 and was solidly built, a former semipro football player. He was the kind of leader that anyone producing a corporate documentary would want to shoot. With his imposing size and outward sweep of self-assurance, he personified "inspirational group leader."

I was still new, so I stood apart from the huddle of men and women in brown uniforms, the 40 or so drivers standing with their hand trucks, handheld computers, and lunch bags, ready to head to their trucks. I stood along a narrow corridor with the other poorly dressed temporary workers. Toward the end of the brief meeting, a chorus of whoops and cheers and what sounded like a military "hua" went up from the drivers. Together with the brown uniforms and specialized embroidered garments that some wore, there was a distinct military feel to our crew.

Looking out at the group of mostly men massed around a clean-cut, well-groomed leader like Pedro, I could not shake the feeling that we were soldiers going into battle, a squad preparing for a mission; that we were a brand army and I was a foot soldier on the front lines. Pedro yelled, "Okay, let's go!" and we made for our shiny brown package-laden vehicles. As the drivers all started their engines and pumped their gas pedals, the high-ceilinged space filled with smoky exhaust and you could smell and taste the adrenalized martial energy, the essence of UPS.

DURING AND AFTER college as I put in time working at television stations, reporting for newspapers, serving magazine internships and otherwise apprenticing myself to the craft of writing, I lived with a strong belief that when I eventually had the freedom to write about the subject that most interested me, I would set out on the road. Traveling to far-off locales and crossing mountain ranges, I would follow a model set out in the books that filled my expanding armchair adventure library: that of a protagonist who lives a mediated, rehearsed, and settled life but pushes out into uncharted terrain to challenge himself and adjust the pending status quo. In this future, I would send dispatches back from expeditions as life-altering and character-testing as Ernest Shackleton's and rambles as far-reaching as Wilfred Thesiger's. I was hardwired with wanderlust, and it seemed appropriate to address that character trait head-on by heading out.

It certainly never occurred to me then that I would find rich material riding around in a delivery truck or standing for hours on end in a fluorescently lit fitting room; that I would end up embarking on a journey to a place possibly considered the most boring destination on earth—the front lines of commerce.

The idea for this journey originated a long time ago. The summer before I started college, I met a kayak instructor who had worked for UPS delivering packages somewhere in the Pacific Northwest. He spoke as enthusiastically about working in howling rainstorms while dressed in UPS brown as he spoke about boating wild spring runoff. For him, working at UPS was as raw and real as climbing peaks and surfing big waves, which probably had something to do with joining a force larger than himself and gaining from the experience; at the time, I wasn't sure. He told me of the days at UPS he had spent trailed by a couple of staff scientists sent out by headquarters to measure anything and everything measurable during the course of his day: the angle in the bend of his knee as he stepped into his truck, the length of time he depressed the gas pedal before engaging the clutch, how far to the left he turned his head to look in the side-view mirror, the average time it took him to retrieve a package from the back of the truck and walk it to a given front door, how long it took a recipient to answer the door after a doorbell button was pressed. Using what is known as time-and-motion study, experts had evaluated him so that they could design systems and tools to make him and his coworkers more efficient, to mass-produce better workers.

For years it was this image of a bearded kayaker that I continued to think about: a guy tracked like a rainforest monkey and measured by a team of experts armed with stopwatches, protractors, yardsticks, and inclinometers. To me, the idea of a human worker as the subject of a corporate experiment stood at the root of something bigger. In it I saw variously the juxtaposition of leisure and commerce, adventure and work, freedom and control. I was intrigued by how a person could be shaped into being an employee and the subsequent role that he or she would play in the marketplace.

It's fair to say that this guy's experience set an idea in my head, an existential itch I needed to scratch. In ensuing years, whenever I neared the UPS building in San Francisco I felt a strange pull inward, a longing for something I couldn't articulate. I later understood my interest to be a deep-seated curiosity, an urge to understand the commercial world that surrounds us by interacting with it in an all-encompassing way, to experience firsthand what it felt like to be a part of an interconnected global workforce by becoming a piece of it. Eventually I knew I had to apply to work for UPS.

So one November, instead of ignoring the pull inward as I rode my bike by the UPS building, I stopped in and applied for a job. Two weeks later, I was riding alongside a driver and delivering packages. The distance from sitting behind the desk in my office to sitting in a rumble seat of a UPS truck delivering packages was surprisingly short. After filling out the application in November, I was invited in for a brief interview, and come December I was in uniform, riding shotgun. Just driving across town to work at the UPS building completely transported me from flat and academic thoughts about brands and corporate culture to actual interactions with live customers and coworkers. The UPS corporate culture, the core values that set UPS apart from other companies, was a huge part of the working experience. After witnessing firsthand that company's strain of culture, I became even more interested in how other large consumer-oriented companies shaped such cultures to make believers out of their own masses of front-line employees.

The ease with which I slipped in under the radar and worked at UPS emboldened me. I came up with the idea of rolling out a similar plan on a bigger scale: setting out on an undercover adventure into the land of retail. I was not so much interested in exposing some form of corporate evil, but in exposing the workplace: what it felt like to work at a few companies and what culture, if any, was handed down from the top or grew organically from the bottom.

As a customer I'd been on the front lines regularly but never seen what went on behind the "Employees Only" signs. I was most curious about the kinds of jobs in which you were meant to dress, act, and behave like your coworkers—either by following clearly defined corporate rules or by participating more informally in a deeply embedded corporate culture.

As the project took shape, I sought to find out what it would be like to switch from my usual role as a customer to that of an employee, from my place as a "knowledge worker" to that of a "service worker." I wanted to know whether the strong corporate cultures that companies bragged about were really as great as advertised, whether the foot soldiers serving vast brands were somehow made more of plastic than flesh, and how front-line employees are molded into certain ways of thinking, acting, and working. I wanted to know how someone like myself, as restless and filled with wanderlust as I am, would respond to an environment antithetical to the one I imagined to be my natural habitat. I wanted to jump right into the fertile workplace Petri dishes where things such as conformity, belonging, and forced belief—things I normally avoided— were thriving.

I would infiltrate and gain membership as a front-line worker, observing from the ground floor, not the boardroom. I would study at close view workplaces that had broken human toil into two chief components: (1) satisfying workers' needs for both "spiritual" and financial well-being and (2) leveraging human effort to create a positive customer experience. I would witness two main things: how companies as varied as the Container Store, Home Depot, and Starbucks bring in outsiders and how I responded to those corporate cultures and their institutionalized attempts to make me conform to them. The goal of the project would be to work among people living the realities of an executive's management directives, yet at a far remove from the person who issued those directives; to wade deep into the retail ecosystem and get a better sense of the people helping the customers, the grunts on the front lines of commerce; to understand what it felt like to have my own beliefs compromised, pushed, and pulled in new ways.

The only way to understand the pervasive world of commerce was to explore it as if it were an untouched stretch of wilderness. By going native, I could see how a handful of companies turned out good people as efficiently as widgets and shaped people into moving parts that allowed the corporate machine to roll along. By wearing their uniforms and joining their huddles—playing a part—I could better understand the modern corporation and its employees.

Initially I was most interested in just what the kayaker had described to me years before, how he had been measured in a hundred ways. In pioneering studies of workers' on-the-job movements in the 1880s, Frederick Winslow Taylor had analyzed tasks and broken them apart into a series of repetitive motions, each of which had to be done in a specific way, in a given time frame, and using appropriate tools. Taylorism shaped modern management theory and the development of the postindustrial workforce. But work today addresses an additional set of issues that drew my interest more than any others: the mental makeup of workers and their drive to join and believe in a particular work endeavor. The new "retail environments" and "store experiences" that increasingly surround us and draw us into daily interactions demand more of workers than the mechanical work that Taylor studied to develop theories on work efficiency. There is a new aspect to the scientific management of the last century: If good service is the goal, moving x shovelfuls of sand per hour is not enough; something else has to come into play. Beyond studying workers' movements, some companies had come to study their minds, to find better ways to win them over, to make them believers. I sensed a new idea in vogue, that if workers created something of meaning for customers, they would in turn find meaning in their jobs and in their lives. This change in the set of demands seemed like it might require a new level of commitment on the part of the worker.

In the military, the front line is the border between two opposing armies; in retail and service companies it is the invisible divide between customers and employees. The thousands of daily interactions out on the wide-reaching front lines of commerce have huge implications for the success of any company, and employees who believe in what they are doing give a company a better chance to succeed. Any company can master the clean, efficient production of goods, but it's harder to manufacture and build loyal employees. People are dirty, sloppy, organic, lazy, envious, rebellious, and real; they get sick, are prone to accidents, and can be independent-minded. They are, in short, human. You would hardly know this, though, because most reports about the workplace distill workers into data points relevant only to investors and economists: retail sales figures, turnover rates, jobless counts, retention statistics, unemployment claims, same-store sales. These numbers don't capture the sense of culture and belonging, the human dramas unfolding in the workplace. It was precisely that human element that I sought to witness as I forged into these work cultures.

An expedition into a series of highly controlled workplaces offered a chance to explore an extremely scripted working life. As I signed on with companies such as Gap and Starbucks that pushed some of the stronger agendas and treated recruits like members of "brand armies," I knew that as a resolute nonjoiner I was the least likely person to find myself in these positions, that part of the adventure would be in charting my own psychological responses as I took on various jobs. The project would be a prank of sorts but also an attempt to move past being typecast as a business journalist by looking into subjects I was truly interested in—corporations, people, work, consumerism—in a truly non-business journalist way.

As I embarked on the journey, I found that transferring between jobs altered not only my view of commerce but also my view of geography. Each job allowed me to see the same world differently. A homogeneous cityscape quickly transformed through my fresh engagement with it. Serving as a conduit from countless warehouses to individual residences as I delivered packages for UPS allowed me to see the movement of material goods in a new way. The facades of buildings shifted as I opened doors and entered hundreds of houses and apartment buildings as if working my way through a life-size cardboard Advent calendar. As I assumed more roles in the commercial sphere, my interest in the act of working became secondary to an attempt to understand better how we experience modern life, a probe of the many ways we operate as we ship parcels here and there, drink expensive blended coffee drinks, and dress ourselves with fabrics designed in urban America and sewn together in India.

Halfway through the journey, I came across a statement that captured the spirit of the project quite well. In the formative years of UPS, its founder, James Casey, was known to repeat a basic phrase: "Anybody can deliver packages." It was both modest and profound, with clear implications: Anybody can deliver packages, *so we had better be the best at it. . . .* Anybody can deliver packages, *but not just anybody can do it like we do.* It's the same sentiment, really, at any leading company: Anybody can pour a cup of coffee, rent out cars, sell pairs of jeans. Except, of course, they can't. The places, it seemed to me, that are the best at these things take "anybodies" off the street and make them their own "somebodies." This completely intangible transformation of individuals is something increasingly critical to the success of companies. By organizing and running a small, yearlong experiment with myself as the subject, I would see and feel this transition in process. The journey would be this: I would walk in as an anybody and depart as a somebody. Or at least that was the idea.

At one memorable point in what became this undercover adventure, as I was applying for a job at Starbucks, a UPS driver double-parked on the street and came in with a medium-size box. He somehow lost his grip on the package and it tumbled to the floor behind the counter.

"I hope that there wasn't anything fragile in there," the manager said in a passive-aggressive tone.

"Me, too," said the UPS driver, hopefully.

It was a symbolic moment. Each of them, stripped of their uniforms—he, a pair of brown pants and a brown shirt; she, a green apron, a black blouse, and black pants—was just a person. But dressed as they were, they each represented a large, multibillion-dollar corporation, a product, a brand, a way of doing things. They were both actors on a vast commercial stage. Off he went, and then off I went. I was still wearing the comfortable and anonymous uniform of the unbranded citizen, but not for long.

ONE

THE OTHER ARMY

A fter the call came inviting me to interview at UPS that November, I drove over to the building. I was directed to a snack
room, where I joined a dozen other applicants, and together we sat
in silence. Soon the local head of human resources, Jed Barnes, entered the room to give us an overview of the job. He had salt-and-
pepper hair and was of medium muscular build. Those of us hired
would ride shotgun in a truck to help reduce the amount of work
for each driver during December's uptick in package movement.
Barnes emphasized that it would be a fun and "energetic" job.

He handed out a job description with a checklist that reduced
our required set of skills to a surprisingly specific group.

*You have to be able to: Illustrate spatial awareness; Read words and
numbers; Concentrate; Memorize; Recollect; Identify logical connections and determine sequence of response; Process up to two or three
steps ahead.*

The sheet noted that we would handle packages of up to 150
pounds and that the average package weighed 11 pounds. Barnes
cautioned that we would be exposed to the season's inclement
weather and that we had to like that in a job.

As he told us that UPS would supply us with uniforms, I stifled a smile—if I was going to go undercover, I wanted to look and feel the part. He said we would be paid $8.25 an hour and charged a union fee. He then handed out applications.

Before I joined UPS, I felt that I knew a fair amount about its brand, one that had held up remarkably well for decades. The image of this company in my mind was one where solid customer service and cutting-edge technology reigned, where the customer was always right, and where there was tremendous goodwill between customer and company, personified by its eager and enthusiastic, competent drivers. Like many others in the room that day, I had been exposed to global UPS advertising that recast the company simply as *Brown* and asked, "What can Brown do for you?"

UPS used that tagline in everything from recruitment advertising to prime-time TV ads, reaching both internal and external audiences. By extolling the importance of the organization to the world at large, UPS gave its employees a rallying cry, a connection to the brand, another reason to want to be a part of UPS. There was an unstated equation that also shaped how the UPS troops thought of the company: *UPS = Brown→Brown = me→I am Brown →What can we do for you?*

Whereas the relative newcomer FedEx was known mainly for the speed of its deliveries ("When it absolutely, positively has to be there overnight," declared its classic slogan), UPS was known for the care and responsibility with which it delivered. I wanted to know what it felt like to wear the brown uniform—to *be* Brown.

As I filled out my application, I struggled to make my real employment background fit into the boxes on the form. I stated that I had been mostly self-employed and listed a friend who could vouch for several years of self-employment. My main goal was to not raise any red flags, to sneak in unchallenged; knowing that I would do the required work, I was not concerned with falsifying my work history.

After we completed the paperwork, we were called next door, one by one, into a cluttered conference room. Barnes's colleague Lou, dressed in a cheap blue suit, was lower in rank and less articulate than Barnes. He asked me why UPS should hire me.

"I am responsible, and I'll work well as a team player with the driver. I am fit," I told him. "As a customer of UPS, I am a big fan of the brand, and I think that working here will be a good experience. I am available during the dates you would need me." And that was the extent of our dialogue. I got a call about five days later asking if I was still available and interested. I said yes and was told to come in the following week for a four-hour orientation.

My first day on the clock was this half-day orientation, which was loosely broken into four segments: filling out more paperwork, getting a security briefing, learning how to use the UPS handheld field computers, and listening to a safety overview in which our group checked out the inside of the iconic brown trucks for the first time.

Although most people think the approachability of UPS's drivers is one of the company's stellar qualities, we were given only a brief lesson in how to treat customers. It went something like this: If a customer is angry at you or upset that a package has not been delivered, tell them that you are sorry. Do not confront them or engage them.

The local UPS loss-prevention director came in and stared at the dozen of us filling out forms. "It takes a lot of paperwork to get a job at UPS," he said, "but very little paperwork to lose your job here." He told us that we were not to open boxes or look inside them, and that we could not conceal anything in our pockets.

We were paired up, handed a delivery information acquisition device, or DIAD, and taught how to use it. The clipboard-size computers were covered with buttons and had small screens and a user interface that was not intuitive. We practiced entering information about a hypothetical delivery, and I quickly got lost. The boards we would have in the field, we were told, were the newest technology and would allow us to move on autopilot; simply scanning bar codes would be the drill.

Bruce, the tall, skinny, middle-aged manager who had shown us how to operate the DIADs, offered some advice. He'd worked as a driver years before, he said, and the winter months could be cold. He suggested packing an extra set of socks and changing into them at lunch. Just having warm and dry socks after lunch, he said, made a big difference. It was simple advice, really, but to us it was more: It was proof that people like Bruce who had done time in the field could move up in the organization. Later, I learned that the average UPS manager has been at the company 16 years and has held seven different jobs with the company.

Safety training was basic. We were taught by a big guy who wore a green button-down shirt and who seemed to be teaching for the first time. Though he talked for a half hour, we learned little. Bend your knees and exaggerate your lifting, we were told. "This will save your knees and back in a few years' time." We were told to take a three-point stance (feet planted and arm out) and use the handrail to enter and exit our trucks. Our seasonal jobs were to last only a month, so we were getting a similarly abbreviated introduction to the company.

We went downstairs to find an empty delivery truck. Each of us self-consciously practiced entering and exiting the truck cab, and then we gathered in the back of the truck, which we were told was called a package car (a term I would never again hear at UPS). There was something special about entering the truck's sanctum sanctorum, with its aluminum shelves and a top covered with translucent Mylar to let light in.

Accountants have tax time, smoke jumpers have high fire season, and teachers have back-to-school. For those in the package-delivery business, nothing is more hectic than the end-of-the-year holiday season, the period from October through December 24, known as prime time or the Christmas rush. To face down a seasonal workload spike of up to 200 percent, UPS hires part-time employees during this period each year. To best understand UPS—the brand, the company, the culture—December was the time to go inside.

MY FIRST DAY on a truck was a Monday. I drove to UPS headquarters, a fortress of freight, a blockwide fixture in the San Francisco landscape. I'd seen the building my whole life but never entered it. Once I was inside, Lou from human resources took me to get a uniform and then pointed me toward the locker room, where I changed out of my street clothes. The uniform had four pieces: a pair of basic brown work pants that fit a little too snugly; a short-sleeved collared shirt with epaulets and buttons down the front, cut short enough that you couldn't really tuck it in; a thin brown cotton pullover; and a nonlogoed brown wool beanie. I had the locker room to myself, and after buttoning up my shirt, I took a second to stare into the mirror. I was about to leave my current life. As I changed into this new brown uniform, I was changing my attitude. I was becoming one of them.

Lou walked me to another room. I pulled up a chair behind two guys plugging away on computer keyboards. They sat in front of six glowing screens and were tracking packages, talking with drivers on the radio, sending text messages, and fielding occasional complaints from customers. Within seconds they were able to find the exact package a customer was calling about. "Yeah, sure, Miss West, we will redeliver that package for you tomorrow. . . . No, no problem at all." Sitting there, I found myself already making an attitudinal shift from being the whining customer on one end of the line to being the guy doing his job as best he could.

The UPS Sunset Center was the subgroup of employees in the UPS San Francisco operations that I was joining, and the unit was responsible for delivering packages to a rectangular swath of San Francisco that ran right through the middle of the city, roughly from the westernmost side, through downtown, to the Bay. A half hour passed before a manager named Eve gave me a ride to Twin Peaks, the two hills that stand domelike in the middle of San Francisco, to meet a driver named Jim, who was in the middle of his shift driving a route and delivering packages. Despite having lived in San Francisco most of my life, I had only a vague sense of where I was when Eve pitched me into Jim's truck, parked among the squat pastel stucco houses of San Francisco's western neighborhoods. I would soon gain a thorough knowledge of the area and build an intimate relationship with the windswept urban topography of this delivery route.

As a customer, I had never thought much about how a company like UPS organizes its deliveries or deploys its drivers. On the ride to Twin Peaks, Eve explained that UPS, like the post office, breaks its delivery territories into routes. Each driver is responsible for a specific route, where he or she gains local knowledge and builds customer loyalty. With a typical load of 180 packages, a driver might cover a route of 20 square blocks or five square miles, depending on the population density. During the holiday season, however, as routes necessarily shrink in proportion to the increase in package load, UPS needs more trucks on the road. Seeing the patterns and organization behind the UPS delivery system was like learning for the first time that birds migrate south in winter, that underlying organizational principles control phenomena you once viewed as random.

Not comfortable yet in my new brown uniform and still clueless about how the DIAD that I held actually worked, I was a bit uneasy when I met Jim. But he blunted my concerns with an open, friendly smile and steady chatter. Together we made a quick delivery, the first and last time I would be shadowed by a driver. I tentatively pressed the right buttons on the handheld and got the customer's signature onto my board as Jim looked on approvingly.

Jim Ulugia was a large guy of Samoan descent. He weighed upward of 300 pounds but carried his mass with finesse. His exaggerated features gave him the look of a pulp comic-book character. Despite the rainy season of early winter, Jim sported UPS-issue brown shorts and a pointy embroidered UPS-logo ski hat. He was a talker, an optimist. He was fond of the phrase "There you go!" as a response. And he tended to punctuate his sentences with the word *dude* frequently, with good effect. Later I heard other drivers call him Big Jim or Jimmy, and it was clear that he was a leader among the drivers and a critical link between management and workers.

Big Jim was the perfect person to work with on my first day. He was not just a guy with a job, he was a passionate worker, a true UPS-er. He was focused intently on life unfolding around him. He was loud and proud, a driver whom customers would not forget. And for me, he became a sort of big brother. I saw him just about every morning and had lunch with him a few times in the field. He said nice things about me to other drivers and to managers; he sang my praises and watched over me. If there was anyone to set an example for a new worker, Big Jim was the man.

Riding alongside him, I had a great vantage point, a view from the front lines. Jim asked few questions about me but freely shared his own story. He said that friends in the police department had recently talked to him about joining the force, and he had given it some thought. He was the first one in his family to buy a house. He'd purchased it in a planned community and taken photographs of every phase of building, from the stakes-in-the-ground stage on. He now lived there with his wife and three kids and commuted

over an hour each way to work. Driving far into San Francisco
from communities where they could afford homes was typical for
UPS drivers. In an overall economy of constant job movement, they
were an incredibly loyal group. Jim had worked at the company for
just two years, but most drivers I met had clocked 10, 15, even 20
years.

After a handful of stops, Jim and I cut out for lunch, angling a
half-mile over to the local Safeway deli for some sandwiches and
chips. We took our food out to eat in the truck and were soon
joined by another truck with an Asian driver named Roger and his
helper, Nico. The conversation had only one topic: the women we
delivered packages to, drove by, or otherwise happened to notice on
our route. It was not demeaning or entirely politically incorrect. It
was male bonding, yes, but it was also recognition of these drivers'
role as "UPS guys" in the greater world. They knew the attraction
many women had to them or to the image that they projected as
men in brown—service providers. They knew their worth and
flaunted it. After lunch, a union-mandated hour, Jim and I set off
to make the rest of our stops.

Because he didn't have seniority, Jim covered for drivers who
were sick, on vacation, or out on disability. Drivers are just one
group of workers at UPS, but they are the top of the internal food
chain. In a desirable city like San Francisco, you need to work your
way up to become a driver. Jim was covering for Carolyn, who usually drove that route, but he still knew quite a lot about the people
living in the area. I found it strange to suddenly be the face of UPS
to customers who did not know that I was a temporary worker.
Customers, many of whom were oddly enough home in the middle
of the day, had no idea that I had started my job mere hours
before.

UPS technology made deliveries fairly easy. Jim and I each carried a DIAD. These machines, about the size and weight of a heavy

notebook, had our route programmed and allowed us to easily scan packages as we moved from truck to stores and houses and back. By simply scanning bar codes on packages, we were tied into a global technology back end filled with millions of data points, able to do our job effectively on the front end.

After lunch, Jim and I cranked through more than 150 stops. In the late afternoon, when my energy flagged, Jim shared a bag of Mother's white and pink iced sugar cookies with me. With the last of our packages dropped, early winter darkness fell. We pulled over for a few minutes to look from high on Twin Peaks eastward toward the Bay Bridge and over the city sparkling below. "Dude, I wish my wife was here instead of you," Jim said.

At 6:30 Jim thought it was early enough in the evening that if we headed back to "the building" (as everyone called our headquarters), we'd definitely be sent out to make more deliveries. He voted to head over the hill to "the Haight and the Ashbury," as he called it, where he had worked the route before and knew a lot of the store owners and managers. We drove down Haight Street, our doors pulled open in the cool December air, with Jim yelling out at shop owners. "Hey, Mary, Mary!" "Yeah! Will!" It was a level of connection I had never witnessed—that of retailer and UPS driver. We were pretty much wasting time, though seen through another lens we were spreading UPS cheer up and down the street.

Working with Jim that day was tiring enough to send me to bed early when I got home. The next morning, I got to the building by 8:15 and changed into my uniform. As I was talking to Jim, he turned to a supervisor walking by. "We were out crushing it yesterday," he said. "That's what I heard," the supervisor replied. I felt like I was joining the team.

RIDING ON THE BROWN TRUCK

On my second morning I went into the field with a driver named
Carolyn, for whom Jim had been covering. At first glance Carolyn
defied the UPS deliveryman stereotype. She was tall, skinny, white,
and in her late forties. She was immediately pleasant and even a little
flirtatious. It was a cold day, and once we were in the truck she pulled
out a jacket that she said I could use, a two-ply coat with a quilted
vest zipped in. She also gave me a traditional-looking brown UPS
baseball cap. It was a step up from the uniform I had been issued, and
I was immediately grateful for her generosity. I filled the pockets
with UPS-logo ballpoint pens and delivery-notice pads. I wanted to
look good, or at least to look like the more seasoned drivers. On the
way through the building, I had been surrounded by other drivers
who wore the uniform every day and had the swagger that comes
with knowing how you look and how to wear each piece of clothing.
There was an ideal, and I wanted to at least try to hew to it.

The next day I was on the same route, working again with Carolyn. I had no yardstick with which to measure the difficulty of the
job or our particular route, but I found the work to be physically
demanding. We worked from 8:30 AM, when we left the building,
to about 7:30 PM. Rain came and went all day, dripping on us as we
walked from the truck to houses and apartments, and the wind
blew sideways across the urban ridgelines. I found that the weather
determined the mood of our driving and delivering: When the sun
shined into our steel-and-glass cockpit, we had fun—we were on
task, purposefully moving through our day. But when it was cold
and rainy and I was huddled into my jacket, trying to keep the
DIAD dry and the scanning glass free of raindrops, the job was a
grind. By 10 that night, when I'd gotten home, showered, eaten
dinner, washed my uniform, and sat down to take a few notes, my
muscles ached and I was completely exhausted.

On my fourth day we had a ton of packages, and we made almost 200 stops—200 times unbuckling the seat belt, stepping out, delivering a package, getting back in the truck, and rebuckling. As the day progressed, we could see how many stops were left by paging down on the screen of the DIAD boards we carried everywhere like electronic appendages. By day four, the novelty of the job was fading fast as the reality of manual labor settled in.

At about 5 PM, as it got dark, we got some help from two other drivers who backed their trucks up to ours, bumper to bumper, and helped us balance our remaining load so that the packages would get delivered that day. The rest of the year, by comparison, is more manageable. December is a time of sacrifice for all members of the UPS workforce, a collective push to reach the finish line that is Christmas. During that busy season, once you completed your stops, the protocol was to call into the building before driving back, to make sure you were not needed to help another driver. That system was interesting from an efficiency perspective. Everyone was wary of calling in too early and getting sent out again, so some people screwed around until a certain hour passed—maybe 6:45 or 7:20, depending on the night. The upside was that if you had a huge amount of work, you knew other people would come to your aid. The system reinforced the fact that though you might have felt that you were on your own, you were, literally at the end of the day, part of a team. By 6 PM, it was pitch black and raining as Carolyn and I dropped the last dozens of packages in dark doorways.

I had no idea at the start of the day, but my fifth day on the job would be critical. The evening before, I had been crushed—physically and mentally. The driver named Roger whom I had met on the first day had mentioned that few helpers last longer than four days on the job. It sounded ludicrous at the time but totally realistic by the end of my own fourth day. "I can't tell you how many drivers have come back from lunch and found their helper's uniform draped over their hand truck with a Post-it note saying, 'Sorry, couldn't hang with the job,' " he'd said.

Although I should have been home the night before catching up on sleep, I went to a holiday party and ran into my friend Josh McHugh, a writer with whom I had an office when I was not out on assignment. After playing a defined and undercover role all day, I enjoyed coming out of character and sharing my experiences with people outside of UPS, putting into words the thoughts I had had all day. I told Josh that I was done, that it seemed like five solid workdays would be enough; I'd gotten an idea of what it was like working there, and I was calling it quits. He argued for soldiering on until Christmas, for the sake of the narrative arc of any story I might tell and the integrity of the project, if nothing else. He had just participated in a punishing NASA study to determine the effect of G forces on the human body for a magazine article. "You've run marathons and climbed mountains," he said over a beer. "Just think of this as another exercise in endurance."

Apparently my first-week experience was one that others shared. Later I read in a book on UPS that "experienced drivers vividly recall their first days on the job, when the workload seemed not just difficult but nearly impossible. . . . [One driver] says the best advice he got from the veterans when he started was 'Don't quit at the end of the day. Wait until the next morning.' "

Back at it that Friday morning, I was assigned to another driver, Miguel. Because the loads were still not at peak level my first week, the managers shifted me around to whoever needed help. Unlike Big Jim, Miguel did not seem to be a welcoming ambassador to the brand called UPS, but he seemed resigned to taking me on for the day. Miguel was an angry, fired-up guy. With the truck still in neutral, he pumped the gas pedal up and down, as all around us the other trucks—each parked two feet from the next—did the same. There were more than 25 trucks starting their engines in close proximity, and the sound and smells of exhaust flooded our open doors and the whole building. Miguel pulled out into the line of trucks leaving the building; our line fed into another line, and then we threaded out the entrance. A supervisor, in a shirt and tie, stood in the middle of 17th Street holding back traffic and motioning us out of the building. Brown UPS trucks poured onto the street like bees fleeing a hive. Some turned left, some turned right, all dispersing to deliver to the city's 750,000 residents.

As this was apparently "Accident Free Friday," a crowd of white-collar women from the office part of the building, which everyone called "upstairs," stood in the drivers' sight on the sidewalk waving "No Accident" signs as we pulled out with the other trucks into the streets of San Francisco. Miguel jerked the wheel as the transmission slipped, but he got the truck back into gear before anything happened. "All this talk about no accidents and I get into one right here!" he yelled. "I should run over all of them!" It was clear that at UPS safety was a real issue—another variable to be factored into the overall efficiency equation and drilled into drivers week after week, even if some of them found it silly.

We drove directly toward the Lower Haight. I was excited because it was a retail area, which meant more interaction with people, more material for my study, and a change from the sleepy neighborhoods of the past several days. Miguel wanted to start working immediately, to *get after it* and *hit it hard,* as he said a dozen times. Big Jim had told him I was a good worker, but Miguel didn't trust my skills. It became clear that he was prepared for me to screw up his rhythm, and to be surprised if I actually helped him out.

The first hour we worked together, Miguel moved like a man on the run, looking and acting like he was high on amphetamines. He drove rapidly between deliveries and with such a desperate adherence to forward momentum that I was forced to sacrifice the skilled work I had been practicing by throwing packages at doorways and sprinting back to the cab as he piloted the truck with me barely strapped in. The safety message had clearly made little impression on him.

Throughout the day we double-parked our vehicle and each walked down the block to deliver on our own, meeting back at the truck. As we roared along, I scribbled down Miguel's phrases whenever I could sneak a moment on someone's landing or doorway, or in an elevator of an apartment building. We were definitely hitting it hard. By midmorning Miguel was telling me, "You're a good man, Frankel" and that I was not "like most of the guys" but was "a rare breed" and "better than some of the full-timers." Once he realized that I was a consistent worker who would not, in fact, screw up his rhythm but allow him to work less that day, he confided in me. "Let's hit this shit hard for a half hour and then take our break," he'd say, or "Let's knock this shit out," exclamations punctuated by enthusiastic his-fist-to-my-fist pounding. The teamwork was intoxicating; as I was winning Miguel over, he was pulling me further in. We clicked through dozens of deliveries. Because the computer tabulated how many packages had been dropped and how many were left, I gained a true feeling of accomplishment as we moved.

Together we delivered two large boxes to an attractive young woman who asked us to carry the packages up the stairs to her apartment as she waltzed seductively ahead of us. "You have a very nice Christmas tree," Miguel told her in monotone, motioning to a sparsely lit Douglas fir in her living room. When we were back on the street, Miguel started laughing. "I was thinking sandwich, man. Would you have been into that, Frankel?"

Driving around with Miguel, or any driver, in the clattering diesel truck, it was hard not to look at the largely homogeneous people of San Francisco as a bunch of softies—people walking slowly with yoga mats protruding out of their hipster messenger bags and clutching four-dollar lattes. I knew in my real life I didn't look so different. But today, Miguel and I were part of the city. There was no question that we belonged. We were global but endemic at the same time. We were "UPS guys," a staple of the cityscape. We blended into the fabric of the city like handbill-covered lampposts or overgrown shrubs. We were working and sweating, not just going to meetings, scratching ephemeral notes on whiteboards, and forwarding electronic documents. We were part of a far-reaching, high-tech, and no-nonsense service industry that allowed the city to connect to the larger world.

For lunch Miguel took me to a hole-in-the-wall burger joint that I would never have ventured into on my own. But the food was great and we ate it out in the truck, sitting on a couple of boxes in back. Most drivers made a point of buying their helpers lunch to recognize the assistance we were giving them. Before lunch we made deliveries to a few music-recording studios and to an incense-and-candle store run by a woman Miguel simply called "the hippie chick." Never ready for his deliveries or pickups, she was the bane of his daily route.

After lunch, Miguel got an electronic message from a supervisor named Stu saying that he would come by to pick me up at 2:30 and then drop me off on Carolyn's route. That meant that I had worked hard all day to drop our load only to be taken to another route with an equal amount of work to be done. The managers had figured out how to use me well. I was good at the job and took it seriously, so they realized that they could effectively work me extra hard. Moving me from Miguel to Carolyn was a great way to maximize my utility. I started thinking about how best to quit—whether to call in later or simply to never come back.

When he arrived, Stu said he'd heard I was a good worker. He asked me what I did before working at UPS, and I mumbled something about seasonal telemarketing, then steered the conversation back to the challenge of UPS Christmas operations. I was slightly worried that in tight quarters Stu might out me as a journalist, but the reality was that he didn't care who I was as long as I was helping the team move freight.

The general take on management that I picked up on seemed cautiously positive. I heard more sympathetic comments regarding how poorly some of the managers were treated than spiteful remarks by workers. It was a place, it seemed, where if you did your job well, all would work out for you. It was, however, a physically taxing job. On-the-job injuries seemed common. One temporary worker like me had badly torqued his spinal cord the very first morning he was dispatched into the field.

Like the crescendo of a symphonic work, pieces of the UPS machine would have to work together and unite as one during the climactic second-to-last week of December. The supervisors and managers, such as Stu, were increasingly helping out by making deliveries. They seemed excited to shed their ties and don our brown uniforms, to lose their management affiliation and join the rank and file. Stu explained that most of the year there were about 35 trucks from our center on the road but that during the final week before Christmas, there would be almost 50, each with a helper like me. I'd been checking out the other helpers each morning. They were easy to identify by their slouched posture and cheaper and lower-thread-count (and often baggier) uniforms. Not everyone got "real" clothes from a driver, as I had from Carolyn.

Though most of the year UPS delivers 15 million packages a day, during December it typically delivers 18 million packages during the days leading up to Christmas and up to 21 million around December 20. The number of packages delivered by UPS is in fact used by some economists as an "obscure economic indicator"—such as the number of shipping containers brought into the United States, parking lot rates in particular cities, the price of a Big Mac in various countries—all ways to judge the health of the economy.

Back with Carolyn that Friday afternoon, it seemed to me that hers would be my regular route if I stayed on. It rained off and on all day, and my clothes were damp from a combination of perspiration and precipitation. By the end of that day there was a perceptible emptiness that I could hear and feel in the large space behind us; instead of a crammed compartment of boxes, we sat in front of a hollow, drumlike metal box filled with cold air.

Somehow, rising out of my own sense of exhaustion, that Friday was a good day. I had driven into work certain that it would be my last day, but at some point in the early evening, wired after a cup of coffee and thundering in our truck down O'Shaughnessy Boulevard toward the 280 freeway and then shooting along the dark, wet highway back to the building, I felt a sense of accomplishment at having delivered our hefty load. I decided that I could—that *I had to*—crank it all the way to Christmas Eve.

That day I had moved from being a stranger on the outside to a part of the group, someone on the inside. I had shifted from being an observer to a participant. I started thinking less about my life on the outside and comparing it with being inside. I had pushed myself to the breaking point and decided to leave. And then I was reeled in—not against my will but because I had new feelings that made staying the right thing to do.

NINETY PERCENT UNIFORMITY

There was no doubt in my mind that the uniforms we wore had a galvanizing effect on the workers. I felt a slight, almost magnetic tug when I walked by a coworker similarly dressed, even if we had never met. There was no question who was in and who was out in this group, though I had identified some subtleties. The longer I was at UPS, the more aware I became of the different clothing options.

The uniform I had been issued, with its low thread count, was subpar, more like a dime-store Halloween costume version than the real thing. There were standard-issue clothes that most drivers wore, and then also what appeared to be custom gear such as embroidered sweaters in red and blue, black baseball caps, and visors. Uniforms stood for overall membership, but the custom gear signaled a deeper connection. Big Jim wore a ski hat that he said had been stitched together by the wife of a driver based in nearby San Bruno headquarters. It was a black-market hat, and I wanted one.

Wearing the uniform sped up my own process of inculcation into the UPS culture and served as an indicator of a special bond with the group. The brown we all wore "represents membership in a collective enterprise, commonality over individuality," as Harvard sociology professor Robert Putnam observed. But the uniforms were far from identical, and presented ways to distinguish oneself, even among similarly clothed colleagues. Even seasoned drivers wanted certain articles of clothing, such as Big Jim's ski hat. It was hard to believe that actual UPS workers would be interested in UPS logo clothing; it seemed that such things would be beneath them. But that desire also made sense: If you went to work somewhere every day, you wouldn't want to feel like a drone, a simple knockoff of the next employee. You would want to add your own flourishes. Some went further than others. Years before, I had worked in an office building in San Francisco where we invited our UPS driver to a party. He showed up in a short-sleeved shirt, and after a few drinks, he was persuaded to show off his biceps tattoo—a blue, five-inch-tall UPS logo.

At our orientation, it was made clear to us that we would not receive our final paycheck until we surrendered our uniforms. UPS did not want the uniforms getting into the wrong hands. I'd even heard stories about thieves impersonating UPS drivers to hold up a bank and others burglarizing a highly secure jewelry mart, and there was a growing urban legend about an eBay sale of hundreds of UPS uniforms to a possible terrorist organization. Beyond these apocryphal tales, the garments had genuine street credibility in certain hipster communities. People trying to look cool had long taken to the trappings of blue-collar workers, work clothes you bought at hardware stores—brands such as Ben Davis, Dickies, and Carhartt, built more for integrity than fashion. Among this crowd, the UPS garment embodied an ironic proletarian chic, a form of slumming as old as the preppy habit of wrapping silver duct tape around a pair of Bass Weejuns or L.L. Bean duck-hunting boots. To this crowd, UPS and what it stood for was a flag of authenticity you could wrap yourself in proudly, even though for us, wearing the uniform after work was strictly forbidden in the corporate rule book.

During orientation, we were told rules about personal hygiene and advised to conceal any long hair under a hat and that we could not have any facial hair below our lip. (One guy I'd seen at orientation with a patch of hair under his lip had shaved it by the first day of work.) We were told that we'd have to wear "shine-able" black or brown shoes, and there was even a company-issued shoeshine box near the logistics office. For several days I sported running shoes for comfort until several drivers and a manager encouraged me to find some dark leather boots. UPS is well aware of the strong iconography of its uniforms and the impression that its drivers have walking around wearing them. It knows that each truck and driver in motion creates an image in the customer's mind. The UPS manual dictates that drivers are meant to walk "with a brisk pace" but never to run, because a "brisk pace commands attention, but running requires too much attention" and because drivers are taught to perform other duties while walking.

More than once on the job, I ran into delivery people from FedEx and Airborne, and I was immediately struck by how unimpressive their uniforms were and what these companies were losing in terms of image. The guy from Airborne had long, unkempt hair (not hidden under a hat), a scruffy goatee, and tattoos up and down his arms. His only real uniform was a worn-out blue polo shirt with an Airborne logo and a pair of wrinkled blue pants. I felt like a well-dressed member of an orderly team next to what seemed like his ragtag band.

Jim and Carolyn and many others I met were loyal to UPS, and much of this came directly from the company's culture. As a driver, you are not just someone driving around and dropping off freight all day; you are a *UPS driver*, one of the few and the proud, as the old Marines slogan had it. Absurd though it might have been, I came to feel that even in my ridiculously low-level position, I had been carefully chosen like a varsity soccer team member or a fraternity brother. There was an ineffable feeling that we were doing something bigger than simply dropping off boxes. This feeling clearly started somewhere deep within the organization and then refracted outward as if through a prism and was passed along to coworkers by people like Jim. A culture like this propagates by using an overarching set of guidelines for proper behavior and then having one person imitate another person and pass along certain traits, some of them prescribed from the top, some not. UPS was a place with a palpable spirit, a place where we wanted to be working, where we were made to feel like that chosen few. But it wasn't as if all drivers came from the same mold, and I saw this clearly in two of the drivers I worked with.

Where Jim was loud and optimistic, Carolyn was more reserved and cynical. While Jim drove an hour-plus to work, Carolyn lived less than a mile from her route. While Jim met other drivers for lunch at noisy diners, Carolyn ate at home every day and packed tofu sandwiches for snacks. While Jim favored the saying "There you go!" Carolyn punctuated sentences with the occasional "*oy vey*," spoke French, and once pointed out a doorbell that played France's national anthem, "La Marseillaise." Where Jim played fast and loose with the rules about how far off your route you could drive on break, Carolyn sought to stay on course and worried about getting caught for veering a quarter mile off-route.

When Carolyn talked about a manager quietly riding with her for three days in the rumble seat that I now occupied, the idea that she thought I was a spy from corporate crossed my mind. She talked about guys driving in unmarked cars and videotaping drivers. She told me more than once, in what I thought was a slightly paranoid tone, that management had a book on her that she had seen, a type of detailed employee dossier that catalogued her pluses and minuses, accidents she'd been in, and individualized time-and-motion recordings of her at work. Though we spent hours together every day, I knew I could not tip my hand and tell her that I really was a spy of sorts, working on my own research project. Carolyn was no poser—she'd worked at UPS for 19 years and had even married another UPS driver. She cared deeply about her job and her customers.

In hindsight, I could see that Jim and Carolyn formed two ends of the UPS driver spectrum yet were both solid workers. There was clearly something in their makeup that prequalified them to work at UPS, such as a knack for organization or a need to be on the move. And to stay at UPS, they had to enjoy the rituals of the particular culture. Both Jim and Carolyn were people drawn to the day-to-day adventure that was UPS. It was clear that management had recognized Jim's potential and his embodiment of the ideals inherent in the culture and then sought to buoy his natural proclivities while elevating him for others to emulate. Jim was more of a torchbearer of the culture, Carolyn a perpetuator, but both were critical to its evolution.

TEAMWORK PREVAILS

During my second week, days started blending together. Because I was working such long days, I felt less and less as if I had two lives. As a result, my daily focus grew tighter on the organization. My life was drive to work, work, eat, drive home, sleep, repeat.

As a temporary worker I had paid a union fee but was hardly a member of the Teamsters, the nation's largest union. Still, I appreciated what the union had done for us workers, especially in terms of break time. After a 15-day strike in August 1997, when UPS lost half a billion dollars in revenue, the company had shifted around the drivers' workday to build in a certain amount of break time per hours worked. Employees had to take this time. Some drivers seemed to chafe against the requirement. For me, the enforced downtime was welcome.

By midday I tended to feel that we had plunged into our own form of *The Twilight Zone* as we spun circles in the truck around Sutro Tower, the orange-and-white-striped radio tower that loomed 977 feet over us and crowns the highest point in the city. By lunchtime, after delivering from one house to the next in a constant stream of dizzying movement, I had lost any sense of what direction we were headed in.

Though all of the packages were sealed in brown boxes or yellow envelopes, address tags revealed their contents. We delivered books from Amazon, furniture from Pottery Barn, and chocolates from See's Candies. We delivered cookbooks from Fanny Farmer, baby cribs from Graco, matching linen place mats from Crate & Barrel, and Razor scooters from Wal-Mart. We delivered boxes and padded envelopes from Lands' End, L.L. Bean, QVC, and HSN. We delivered Styrofoam containers filled with meat from Omaha Steaks. We transported packages related to weddings, new babies, and, of course, Christmas. I carried a lot of heavy Dell computers. I was led to wonder what illegal goods I was helping to move as I scanned packages tied with excessive amounts of twine postmarked from Mexico and strangely lightweight shoebox-size cartons with Humboldt County return addresses.

UPS seemed to be founded on the principle of giving its workers a fair amount of autonomy. It was apparent in the flexibility that permitted people to match uniforms to personal style and in the way that each driver had a fair amount of latitude in making minute-to-minute decisions. This was most certainly a part of the UPS management strategy; if the most prized workers were spending 90 percent of the workday on their own in the field, UPS had to train them to think and act for themselves or the system would quickly fall apart. By giving autonomy to the drivers, you allow them to be stronger individuals who can more naturally represent the brand and serve as the crucial human component at the end of a long chain of cutting-edge technology.

Working the same route day after day was educational. I got to know the streets and the people who inhabited them. I got a sense of what it would actually be like to work the same route for 10 or 20 years, as some drivers do. Dropping off packages in so many houses and apartments all day felt like flipping channels on late-night television, moving through scene after scene. As I got the hang of the job, I began to open my eyes to focus more on what was going on in the places where we delivered. I was particularly struck by the odors in houses with each passing day. After a door opened, it was just a matter of seconds until the condensed smell of the house carried outside toward me, like someone exhaling into my face. I tried to hold my breath, but there was always something in my mind whispering that this one might be different, so I would take in the aromatic puff of air. But four out of five times, it was a malodorous smell of pet urine, mold, dust, or cleaning products, or some combination of them all.

After shifting around onto other trucks for a few days, I was now back with Carolyn. Though some days seemed to go on forever, Carolyn and I worked well together as a team. Usually I ran to the houses while Carolyn found each package in the back of the truck and scanned it into one of the machines so that all I had to do was drop it off. When we were smoothly in motion, our actions became robotlike and our speech became distilled to an acronym-filled discourse in which we used as few words as possible: "Is this walkable?" I'd say, wanting to know if I had to get back in the truck to deliver to the next address. "Did you DR that?" I'd ask, wanting to know if Carolyn had already scanned a "driver-released" package so that all I had to do was drop it in a doorway without getting a signature. "Is it sheeted?" I'd ask, wanting to know if it was scanned into a DIAD. And Carolyn might say, "No, that package is NI2," which meant "not in for a second time," that we had tried to deliver that non-DR-able package twice and that on a third attempt we would leave a final notice that the package was being held at the UPS building. Or maybe a customer had left us an SDN, a signed delivery notice, so that we could leave a non-DR-able package. My mind constantly thought of ways to further automate our process (using GPS and neighborhood depots, among other ideas), but doing so would largely defeat the critical human element of our jobs. You could not push efficiency to the absolute limit or you would lose the human touch that built loyal customers.

One afternoon Carolyn told me the story of a former driver in our building. This guy was able to drive and deliver packages with such alacrity and efficiency that he regularly finished his day by two in the afternoon. He went off to another job each day, and his managers clocked him out in the evening. Apparently this went on for years until a newly arrived manager halted the practice and punished those involved. After hearing the story, I tabulated our average stops-per-hour rate and realized that even the two of us were hard pressed to match that driver's speed of 40-plus drops per hour.

Working for UPS, I realized that a corporation's culture is something not necessarily perceived, except by outsiders like me. There were no specific moments when you could say: "I am now joining this culture." Culture is many things, even the story of that superhero driver (that may or may not have been true). To function, the culture had to be organic and move of its own accord. People had to *believe* without being persuaded to do so. Having a culturally specific language certainly helped build employee buy-in. Once, as I threw an NI2 package into the back of our truck, Carolyn joked: "Hey, every package is a guest of honor!" She was channeling some management directive, and it was funny to us both, but she was also translating culture through language-based memes, as Stanford business school professor Chip Heath would later explain to me. Once the corporate minders pulled something out and identified it as a part of the culture, it immediately lost its authenticity. Evolution of the culture was crucial, and to evolve meant to change. As a new worker, I had to feel that I could not only join the culture but also add to it. Yes, UPS prescribed a number of ways of behaving, but the culture flourished on top of this and affected workers throughout the ranks.

This very notion of corporate culture was perhaps best defined by the CEO of IBM, Thomas Watson, Jr., who in a speech in 1962 called culture the "basic philosophy, spirit, and desire of an organization," which "have far more to do with its relative achievements than do technological or economic resources, organizational structure, innovation, and timing." The prevailing view still holds that companies with strong cultures succeed (as opposed to success leading to strong cultures).

Most corporate culture research analyzes artifacts a worker encounters in the workplace: the design of the physical environment, language, technology, products used or manufactured, clothing styles and dress codes, modes of communicating, emotional displays, myths and stories told about the organization, shared and public lists of values, observable rituals and ceremonies. In general, experts who study culture seem to agree that there is an identifiable culture in every company that is not easily assayed by a casual observer and not easily copied by a competitor.

I was struck by Carolyn's deep knowledge of the people she delivered to. She knew the basics, such as whether people were likely to be home and the best places to leave packages if the residents were absent. Long before we had arrived at someone's front door, she knew if a buzzer was broken and you had to knock. But she also knew specific details about illnesses and deaths in the family, weddings, and newborn babies. These seemingly small connections were not inconsequential—they were crucial to the sustainability of UPS itself. Every such link to a customer puts a personal face on an otherwise anonymous corporation, making the corporation seem like it *is* the drivers, which in some ways it really is. By being friendly and helpful to customers, Carolyn was building the UPS brand. And Carolyn's relationships with her customers were intimate. These were people who let her into their homes and shared their habits. Once you had interacted with someone twice, you were no longer a stranger. If you expanded this concept to 80,000 drivers interacting with, say, 50 customers each day, that would mean four million individual impressions made per day.

As a part of the anonymous, ubiquitous, and trusted UPS corps, Carolyn knew everyone's story along her route. There was the blue-collar guy who wore Pendleton shirts and smoked a lot of pot, liked to talk, and, according to Carolyn, inherited his house and some money and hadn't done much since. There was a guy who wore white gloves to cover profound third-degree burns. There was the charming older woman who lived for the opera. There was a soft-spoken couple who had lost a daughter the previous year; Carolyn had delivered her ashes. The drivers I met were smart and hard-working, and it was clear those not made for the job had been weeded out. Employees usually became drivers after working other jobs at the company, such as preloading the vehicles on the night shift. In many ways, drivers are the elite of the UPS workforce.

We often had occasion to cross paths with letter carriers from the U.S. Postal Service. The USPS, Carolyn said, treated its employees poorly. "That's why they, uh, go postal," she said. It was an interesting contrast between them and us. Yes, they had blue uniforms, trucks covered with eagle logos, and cyclist Lance Armstrong as a spokesman, but they lacked our esprit de corps and any attractant that would pull in and nurture great workers. It seemed to neither have a culture of innovation nor be a place of upward mobility.

In the months after I had moved on from UPS, delivery company DHL rolled out a clever multimillion-dollar ad campaign with the message "Yellow. It's the new brown." In *Forbes*, DHL's marketing chief said of UPS: "The more efficient they are, the less human they are," but this seemed more like posturing than reality. UPS clients, he said, were "starved for human interaction," but that had not been my experience.

While UPS commanded some 80 percent of the $60 billion package-delivery market, Carolyn said FedEx's relatively new ground service and the revived DHL had given UPS more competition. This, she said, meant more management focus on tightening efficiency. And it meant that the workers could feel a fair amount of pressure and increased workloads. You saw it when drivers first looked into the backs of their trucks in the morning and said: "Are you fucking kidding? Look at all those packages!"

On the Friday afternoon of my second week, Carolyn told me that the coming Monday would be a good day to call in sick. She said that UPS manipulates its load amounts, holding back semi-truckloads here and there to even the delivery volume. The company had recently done so, but then some storms had caused delays, and Monday would be an unexpectedly high-volume day. If I was going to make it to Christmas Eve, I might be better off if I called in sick. As I thought about it, it also seemed wise to get off Carolyn's truck somehow, to get reshuffled onto someone else's route. I had learned all I could from her, and the job was becoming an endurance test—just as my friend had suggested. Because I was at UPS with an assignment to comprehend its culture, not simply earn $8.25 an hour, I wrestled with doing what I was told by management versus trying to shape my own experience.

That Monday I did call in sick. I took it easy, enjoyed an unhurried breakfast and read the paper with the sun shining through my kitchen windows. But I also felt that I was letting my coworkers down, that my pullout had changed the global delivery equation ever so slightly and added more work to my colleagues' load.

Once I was back at work, the feeling was of a workforce under siege and allied against a strong but controllable force: the constant flow of packages. It was work as war. The adrenaline pulsing through the ranks and increasing teamwork was as critical to success as the wearing of matching uniforms. There were many things that reinforced the martial feel of the job. The section in the UPS worker's manual on driver delivery and pickup methods specified exact driving details, even instructed drivers to insert the key in the ignition with the right hand while fastening the seat belt with the left to save time. Robert Putnam, the Harvard sociologist, noted the military-like codes of operation at UPS: "Aspects of the company parallel military behaviors and values: not only the brown uniforms worn by all UPS drivers, but careful training in standard operating procedures and a culture of teamwork and loyalty." He attributed that military feel to the military backgrounds of many UPS managers in the 1960s. He didn't mention, though, the sense of purpose that one feels when working for UPS.

That day back, after the morning PCM (prework communications meeting), the manager sent me out with an Asian driver named Joel. Though the variations are imperceptible to most civilians, UPS trucks come in a range of sizes, from 200 to 1,200 cubic feet. Carolyn drove a "seven cube" (a truck with cubic footage of 700 feet), but Joel drove a smaller truck, a "five cube." Once I was belted into Joel's truck, he asked me whether I was a supervisor. My age, upgraded uniform, and general demeanor apparently set me apart.

"Oh, you were with Carolyn most of last week?" asked Joel in highly accented English. He told me that without a helper, Carolyn had been out until 10:30 the night before. I felt terrible for letting her down, even if it had been her suggestion. I had moved far from feeling that I wanted to leave UPS.

Joel and I drove out to San Francisco's sprawling Outer Sunset district, where each numbered avenue looked a lot like the next. Some of the packages in the back of our truck that day had been misfiled, causing us to get disoriented and lose time. Joel seemed embarrassed by our slowness. For the first time since I'd started the job, I took a leadership role, suggesting, after an hour of chasing our tails, that we pull over and reorganize our entire load, something that helped a lot.

Each of the 175 or so packages stacked on the six aluminum shelves in the back of our truck had made its own particular journey across space and through time to our vehicle. Some had merely been trucked from a nearby state; others had been flown from one of the more than 200 countries served by UPS. Many of the Next Day Air packages would have come through Worldport, the state-of-the-art air hub and sorting facility in Louisville, Kentucky.

Our batch of packages would have entered the San Francisco building on semis or been picked up from incoming planes at Oakland International Airport. Once they were fed into the first floor of our building, scanners would take down their identifying marks, homing in on extended ZIP code data. Packages would be placed onto a system of conveyor belts that snake around and up the four-story building. It would be in the early-morning hours by now, and the packages would make their way toward the trucks. The overnight crew of preloaders, each person assigned to several trucks, would sort the packages by hand, placing them in each truck, in an order that matched the geographical plan we would follow that day.

But there we were, lost on our route, ignoring our computer-prescribed line, our automated route-planning system. The infrastructure behind us had for the most part worked, but our overnight preloader had mixed up a few packages. Our six shelves each represented a thousand numbers, from one to 6,000, spaced out of sequence on opposite shelves to ensure that the weight would remain balanced in the vehicle as the day wore on. Our task was to simply move any packages that were out of order into the right places.

As the delivery team, we were moving real matter, not just ones and zeros. When there were glitches, drivers, not technology, were the best at solving them. But occasionally there were problems, and I came to think of these as akin to baseball errors, caused by senders or poorly sorted packages. Though UPS is a technology-savvy company, drivers play a number of critical roles that no technology can supplant. Drivers are the minds at the end of a lengthy and incredibly efficient technology system, and they connect dots that a computer can't by intuiting problems and solving them as they are happening.

Joel and I found our rhythm after lunch. At about 5:30 we passed another UPS truck, and I managed to catch a ride back to base before our entire load was delivered. I got a ride into the building with a gentle, soft-spoken guy named Gabe. He was bringing back some packages mailed for overnight delivery from an outlying UPS

Store. On the ride back, he told me in brief how he had first come
to work for UPS 15 years before, and he used his own story as a soft
sell to present UPS, the career choice, to me, a potential future full-
time employee. I was being tapped to become part of a brotherhood,
all aboveboard and with good intentions. Like me, Gabe had started
out as a Christmas employee. During the dark ride back to base, he
gave me a bro-to-bro pep talk about how to get a job: basically by
busting my ass, as he expected I'd been doing, getting some face
time with a supervisor, and then following up in January.

"It's basically networking," he said. "We've got a former gym
teacher, a musician, someone with a master's degree in engineering—people from all walks of life. We are an equal-opportunity
employer," Gabe said only half jokingly. He explained that after
two years most drivers make $24 an hour, and then time and a half
for overtime. He said that some of the hardworking, young, eager
drivers earned more than $70,000 per year (largely because of over-
time pay), while most full-timers made about $55,000. A veteran
full-timer gets about seven weeks off a year. He painted a picture of
how to gain seniority, first by working as a preloader, starting at 10
PM and working for four hours, and then taking on flexible "cover"
driving shifts, as Jim was doing.

That night as we pulled into the building, we passed an idling
semi, and it struck me that if I hopped in alongside the driver, I
might be able to continue around the world in an open loop, riding
shotgun next to a trucker, then a train conductor, then maybe a
pilot as I followed the stream of packages to their places of origin.
A few days later, on Christmas Eve, my brief but informative undercover tour of duty at UPS concluded. By signing on, wearing
brown, and delivering so many packages, I had been immersed in
the culture and I had come to understand what the job entailed.
But I held on to the idea of following a package as it traveled

around the world, and more than a year after my time on the truck, I was able to travel up the package delivery stream. This time, instead of going undercover, I went the official route and got in touch with corporate communications. They graciously arranged a trip for me to ride with a couple of drivers and to visit Worldport, the company's gigantic sorting facility.

OFF TO WORLDPORT

Large-scale technology systems have both front and back ends. The front end collects input and processes it so that it conforms to specs that the back end can use, and the two sides connect through an interface. When I worked at UPS, I started to see the company as a great big computer system with the humans running around on the front end and huge computers and machines whirring in the background. Though the UPS back end is as high tech as they come, those working on the front end, the front lines, are dressed to appear old-fashioned. It's a visual harking back to simpler times when personal interactions were more common. The back end constitutes rooms of servers and hubs stored in safe, cold places that allow the front end to operate smoothly. The front end is where the human interactions happen. UPS has managed to mesh the human and the technological in such a way that neither overshadows the other. UPS was once a trucking company with technology; now it's a technology company with trucks. But when you are on the truck, you are scarcely aware of this shift.

Having been on the trucks, I wanted to see the technology, the infrastructure that supports the driver. Before touring Worldport, I first stopped in Lenexa, Kansas, at a modest-size sorting facility. Unlike the rainy city I delivered in a year before, rural Kansas was steaming hot, so every driver in the local hub was wearing brown shorts and UPS-issue socks. I could sense the same feeling of adrenaline there that I'd felt back in San Francisco. I spent two days in Kansas, first riding with a feeder driver named Lon, a 22-year veteran who pulled trailers with a tractor all day and touched no actual packages—he just hauled them. Then I drove with a traditional package-car driver named April. Both Lon and April had been handpicked by management and served as great tour guides to the UPS workplace. Lon's job was, to me, mind-numbingly boring— each day moving an average of ten 53-foot truck containers back and forth between the UPS building and a JCPenney warehouse just a mile away. But he was into it. April underscored her love of what she called her "route community," the people she delivered to every day and who did things such as knit afghans for her and send her Christmas cards and who in recent months had been sent to war in Iraq. As a passenger in their trucks, I was reminded how hard it is to understand a job without doing it yourself—that there were limits to what a journalistic interrogator riding shotgun could learn. When I asked April if any teams of scientists ever followed her around as in the story I'd heard before college, she said that every three years an engineering student took measurements of her daily route as a way to set benchmarks. Big leaps in efficiency, she said, were a thing of the past: "They had all that figured out before I was born."

Still, April was keenly aware of time: "Every minute you have to be somewhere," she told me. Most modern-day driver efficiency comes from technology, such as preprogrammed routes keyed to geography and traffic. UPS has moved from studying and perfecting person-level efficiency to perfecting efficiency from the technology side. Drivers are "in trace" when they are following the computer. Other changes had had an impact during her time at UPS, such as the bar coding of packages. "The bar code changed our world around," she said. Though UPS had handpicked April for me to ride with, she was candid about all aspects of her job. She told me her weeks were physically exhausting and she needed Saturday to recover. "Three out of five days are great, and I wouldn't change it for anything," she said. She said it's a hard job for women, but also for men. "I've seen grown men go down crying because of stress," she said. I asked April whether her job resembled the military at all. "You bet," she said. "I call it 'the other Army.'"

To maintain perspective as I traveled for the week, I brought along a self-published 249-page screed against UPS cobbled together some years before by a disgruntled ex-employee named Charlie Kane. In *The Tightest Ship: UPS Exposé*, which I found on eBay, Kane champions UPS founder James Casey but savages the company's modern-day executives. He doesn't so much hate the company as he hates its management, which he likens to the gestapo. The book is a detailed account of a number of his colleagues who lost their jobs. "The camaraderie of the guys was great," one of his friends tells him. "It was like wartime, because it was a war. A brotherhood of battered boys in brown. It was a horrible experience I won't forget for the rest of my life." Kane celebrates drivers, such as one named Spike Fullmer, who "was moving even when he was standing still." He writes: "God bless any guy who has worked for UPS for any amount of time and remains married. It ruined my marriage; it ruined my life!" The book ends with a three-chapter explanation of the three ultimately successful attempts UPS made to terminate him. "The best way to describe UPS drivers," he writes, "is as a baseball team where everyone hits a home run every time at bat except one guy, who just hits a triple. This qualifies him as 'least best' and earns him a trip to the interrogation room."

After two days in Kansas, I watched a team of loaders sort hundreds of Next Day Air packages and pile them into a sequence of shipping canisters. Also known as unit load devices (ULDs), air freight containers, igloos, or cans, these rounded containers made of steel and Plexiglas fill the contours of planes. Ben, a supervisor in his mid-twenties, said his team of five was solely responsible for loading the Next Day Air packages so that Lon and another driver could pull them to the airport. He told me that he had come to memorize most of the nation's ZIP codes, or at least the first three digits of them; he could tell a 606 from a 482 and know that one was Chicago and the other Detroit. Lower-tech hubs depend on employees such as Ben who have the geographical mastery critical to fast sorting—after six months on the job, an employee can master hundreds of ZIP codes.

Lon and I pulled a trailer full of cans toward the airport. At the airport, we backed up to a raised loading platform on the periphery of the airport's cyclone-fenced circumference. The UPS airport facility loaders emerged to unload our cans and drop them onto trailers, which were then pulled out to a couple of waiting brown-and-white UPS 727s, which were flown on to Worldport and other hubs for further sorting. Then I got on a plane myself and flew to Louisville, Kentucky, and on to Worldport.

WHEN I ARRIVED at Worldport at 11 PM, there was a small traffic backup as the members of the evening workforce pulled into several parking lots. I found a place to park and looked up into the black sky. Every 90 seconds, on my right and then on my left, a UPS plane popped out of the night and angled its way diagonally toward the runway. Some were steady, fat-bellied Airbuses, others small, wobbly Cessnas. *Psh-sh-sh-sh-sh-sh-sh-sh . . . swish-sh-sh-sh-sh.* The scent in the air was of sweet-smelling jet fuel. If there was a beating technological heart at the center of UPS, it was in the middle of Worldport. I sat and watched for a half hour in the humid night air before heading inside.

Mark Giuffre was my guide for the night. He'd started as a driver in Manhattan 18 years before and wound up in public relations. Mark and I watched a quick video welcome. "It all comes together right here, right now. . . . It's like producing the Super Bowl every night," said the male narrator. Then Mark took over, enthusiastically and breathlessly rattling off statistics:

The UPS AirPark facility is 3.2 miles in circumference and has an area of 585 acres. Worldport, its centerpiece, is a four-million-square-foot building the size of 88 football fields lined up and was built at a cost of $1.1 billion. Staffed by 5,000 workers each night (75 percent of whom are college students, many of whom get tuition paid for by UPS), Worldport processes 84 packages a second, or 304,000 packages per hour overnight, and a total of 1.3 million packages each day.

Breathe.

With 282 aircraft and 2,800 pilots on 1,900 flight segments each day, UPS is the world's eighth largest airline and consumes 700,000 gallons of Jet A fuel each day. With Worldport the central hub of a globe-size package delivery wheel, a package might fly from here to Anchorage, Alaska, and then on to Shanghai. You can inject a package into the system here at Worldport and reach more than 200 countries and territories and 80 percent of the world's population within 48 hours.

Breathe.

"Are you ready to go in?" We hopped into Mark's pickup truck and went through security before entering the UPS AirPark and then drove out onto the tarmac, which was strewn with planes of various sizes. There were Airbus A300s that can haul 330,000 pounds and Cessnas carrying just 300 packages. There were 727s loaded with eight cans and MD11s stuffed with 32 cans. There were DC-8s, 747-400s, and 767-300ERs. A hundred planes land on a given night, and most planes pull up to one of the massive wings that shoot out of the center of Worldport to unload their cans. Some planes park on the tarmac and are unloaded by fleets of K-loader vehicles that use X-hinges to lower each plane's contents to tarmac level.

Being on the tarmac at 1 AM felt like being on an aircraft carrier during battle. In the calm night wind, the crews were relentlessly efficient as they set incoming canisters on wheels linked up into foursomes and pulled by Tugs tractors to loading docks. In each loading bay, a can was pulled across a black metal floor impregnated with inverted casters; a 2,000-pound can could roll easily on that unique surface. Each can, stuffed and stacked with packages, was unloaded onto a boomlike conveyor belt that fit into the door of the can.

Mark kept reeling off statistics:

Packages typically travel through Worldport in around 13 minutes—from unloading until being loaded into another can, bound for a new destination. Inside the building there are 17,000 conveyor motors that run over 122 miles of moving belts. Worldport handles fully one million of UPS's 15 million packages each day. Most packages channeled to Worldport are Next Day Air parcels, but not all U.S.-based Next Day Air parcels go through Worldport.

Pausing for a breath, he went on:

Fuel is barged up the Ohio River and then piped underground 13 miles to Worldport's fuel tank farm. There are three days of extra fuel at any given time to make up for any problems in the supply chain. More than 90 businesses have moved here to be close to the hub.

We entered the "sortation" building, otherwise known as Worldport. Along the first floor, we walked on the rollerball deck that the cans slide so easily on, watching our step. There are three kinds of packages and three sorting channels in Worldport: the standard parcel system that handles all six-sided packages under 100 pounds; the small sort system that handles all boxes under 10 pounds; and the irregulars sort system that handles often odd-shaped packages up to 150 pounds.

Computers allow "package level detail," and this means that after they are unloaded from the modular cans, all of the one million packages that land at Worldport each day go through a dimensional weight scanner, where they are weighed and photographed. All but 5 percent of packages carry "smart labels," which means they are bar-coded and marked with origin, destination, and shipper data. If the label is not bar-coded or has any problem, its photograph is transmitted to the telecode department, where a crew of data handlers sit behind computers to examine the photos and manually type in a destination ZIP code for these packages with "nonsmart" labels. They have 23 seconds to do so before the package is sent to SEA, the sort exception area, where it is further examined by another human. We dropped by the South SEA, and there were two people casually labeling the occasional nonsmart package before inserting it back into the system. Humans are not in major demand in the largely automated center. Memorizing ZIP code sets is not necessary there. Mark said he could train me in 20 minutes and send me out into the sort as a productive team member. The back-end workers at UPS are much more like factory workers; they have very little in common with the front-line workers.

It is inside Worldport's core building where the magic happens, in all its sheer thumping, churning, purring, technological beauty. There was a feeling of relentless forward flow. On the fourth floor, the only floor where humans work, we found our way deeper and deeper into the center of the building until we came to a metal railing and looked down into a multistoried layering of conveyor belts of varying sizes separated by metal grating, an 80-foot-high black-and-gray canyon filled with a matrix of belts and scanners. A belt moving standard six-sided parcels has "singulators" that slow down and speed up packages to maintain an evenly spaced, single-file order.

By traveling upstream to this place far from the San Francisco streets where I had delivered packages, I had closed the loop. I could finally connect the front end, where I had worked, with the back end. Looking down into the smooth-running machines was like watching a steam-engine locomotive hurtle by on iron tracks, like watching a whale breach or a glacier calve. Watching this highly efficient transfer of goods was like witnessing a natural act. The conveyor belts were tributaries of a river that poured out, from there at the back end out to the front end, out into the ocean of capitalism.

TWO

ONE GREAT EMPLOYEE

After I left UPS and decided to take the project further by working undercover at other companies, I feared I might not have chosen the best time to launch the project. As I waited and waited for managers from Starbucks and a few other companies to invite me in for interviews, I read the *Wall Street Journal* with a new level of interest. My experience was loosely matching that of other job applicants: Labor was down. The *Journal* reported that "non-farm payrolls added just 78,000 jobs in May," which was cited as the worst performance in two years. "Job growth has been on a bouncy ride in the past year," one article noted, "beating economists' forecasts one month and falling short the next. Hiring was anemic across an array of industries. Businesses hired almost no temps, sometimes a bad sign for future hiring." The article quoted an economist who concluded that "the labor market is just not generating much traction."

At the same time, I had a good feeling that the jobs I was looking for were not the kinds of jobs that fit neatly into these traditional labor reports. The employers I sought—such as Starbucks and Home Depot—excelled where others failed, and the specific jobs I was looking for were a step up from low-wage service jobs. The employers I sought pay a premium, and though the premium may be just a dollar or two per hour, it allows them to attract a slightly more qualified employee than those firms that hire the most employees for the lowest amount. I was less interested in employers who treat labor costs as a spot market (as one for oil or coal) and seek to pay the lowest wages possible. Business theorist Peter Drucker split the modern post-capitalist worker populations into knowledge workers and service workers, noting that "service workers, as a rule, lack the necessary education to be knowledge workers." But many of the companies I was aiming for target people on their way to getting the skills to become knowledge workers. These companies generally offer other premiums too, such as health insurance. Despite the cautionary news in the *Journal*, I hit the pavement.

Part of what interested me about companies that relied on front-line employees was the methods they used to decide whom to hire. As I waded further into the hiring stream, I wondered just how companies recruit the kind of person that fits their corporate culture. The recruitment process seemed critical as a means to select the right army to handle the masses of customers and to serve as worthy messengers of a given brand, but in my own cursory attempts to land jobs there seemed little agreed upon means to discern who would qualify.

After I'd worked at UPS, choosing the companies where I would next go undercover was neither wholly random nor strictly scientific. My goal was to isolate a few of the better service companies I already knew as a customer. We all interact with front-line employees every day, whether we are buying a pair of jeans or a cup of coffee, and many of the companies that made my short list were recognized by some external source such as *Workforce Management* magazine or *Fortune*'s yearly "100 Best Companies to Work For" report. Initially I strolled around some stores to observe the retail environment with new eyes. In the end, I applied at those places that just seemed right. One of these places was the Container Store.

While I was in an REI store examining a piece of luggage, a fellow shopper kneeling in the aisle suggested that I could find the same piece next door at the Container Store for $40 less. A few minutes later, I made my way to the store and, oddly enough, encountered the very same guy, who now was wearing the blue-and-white T-shirt and apron of a Container Store employee. He greeted me as if we'd never seen each other. Without missing a beat, he launched into the reasons I should buy the suitcase with its "book-style opening for easy access and packing, built-in laundry chute, external compression straps, and a soft-touch telescoping handle." This guy, it seemed, spent his breaks studying luggage; I soon found out that his compulsive behavior was common among Container Store workers.

Three weeks after applying at the Container Store, I found myself seated on a folding chair in a circle with 10 other applicants for a group interview. We were a crew of good-looking, handsomely dressed adults in our twenties and early thirties. Each of us had received a call inviting us to come in for an interview. We each wore a name tag. Our circle was stationed in the middle of the mezzanine of the San Francisco store, and customers were free to wander around us and take note of a sign that explained: "Now interviewing neat people."

In the course of the project, I found that the group interview—to which a store hiring crew invited its top candidates and got to watch them interact with one another—was an increasingly popular technique. Before the interview at the Container Store, I had wondered how the group dynamic would unfold, whether there would be vigorous intragroup competition, and how I might come out in the end.

Our group sat in the bored, anticipatory silence that I was getting used to in such situations. We each found a store catalog on our chairs, and I stared at the pictures as I waited for the interview to begin—aspirational images of idyllic large pantries; garages not overcrowded like mine and instead hung with small, clean shovels that had touched no dirt; vast walk-in closets that displayed clothes as museum pieces; spartan kitchens; family rooms loaded with art supplies of every kind and many useful drawers in which to hold them.

Pete and Kim, two Container Store employees, joined our circle and started the interview. They introduced themselves and took a few minutes to tell us how they had come to work for the company. Kim was a friendly, slightly pudgy woman in her late twenties with a mane of blond curls and rosy cheeks. She had a maternal, welcoming smile. She had quit her job as an elementary school teacher in Boston and moved to San Francisco two years earlier. She had walked by the store, checked out the window display, and applied. She started as a part-timer and within six months went full time. Her family members worked in education and at non-profits, not in retail jobs, she said. She believed the Container Store was a great place for her and, not for the last time, referred to the notion of retail as a respectable career. One couldn't help but feel excited for someone who had found her path in life the way she said she had.

Pete was six feet tall and toned. He had cropped black hair and a soul patch. He wore tight, faded blue jeans and a standard-issue black Container Store shirt rolled up over his biceps, where tattoos peeked out. Around his neck he wore what looked like a tribal leather choker, and he wore matching brown leather bracelets on both wrists. Pete had come from Costco, the wholesale supermarket chain, and he said clearer workplace communication and a better ability to grow as an employee were two advantages he had found at the Container Store.

Pete and Kim asked us to introduce ourselves and share what had brought each of us to the Container Store. I was the first to go and told everyone that I liked to be organized and wanted to share that interest with customers. The 10 of us interviewees included a woman who had just enrolled in a graduate program in psychology, an immigrant from the Philippines who had worked as a chemical engineer, a master's student in social work, and a full-time nanny who identified herself as a craftswoman.

One of the applicants, Elizabeth, was a preppy woman in her early thirties dressed in the suburban uniform of slip-on clogs, a pressed white blouse, and pedal-pusher khaki pants that exposed her ankles. She described coming in a few weeks before with her mother to shop for new shelving and other equipment for her new apartment. Without being too obvious, she showed that she was a dedicated shopper.

Joyce, in her late twenties, was studying for a social work degree. She recalled buying a backpack a few weeks before. When she had asked the salesperson just how much the backpack could hold, that salesperson, along with another, had run around the store finding heavy items to slip into the backpack. Pete said he remembered sitting in the break room eating lunch and watching on the store's closed-circuit video monitors as his coworkers trotted around with a stuffed red backpack.

My fellow interviewees were enthusiastic and talked knowledgeably about shopping experiences at the Container Store. At other interviews I had felt as if I had to be quiet and reserved so I wouldn't stand out as being too articulate or passionate. But at the Container Store I felt as though I would have to present a polished, honest version of myself if I were to make it to the next round. The Container Store wants to hire die-hard customers, so its hiring practices remove the traditional wall between customers and em-

ployees and celebrate the employee as customer. By doing this, they
cut out the us-and-them divide that pervades employee-customer
interactions. It made sense to interview us right on the sales floor.

After everyone had shared their reasons for coming, Kim told us
many facts that I dutifully copied into the pages of the catalog on my
lap. The three key differentiators at the Container Store, she said,
were the number of products sold (more than 10,000), the elfa brand
shelving system (the "ultimate organizing product"), and a guiding
credo that said "service equals selling." Kim described selling as a
team exercise at the Container Store: "We sell solutions to problems."

Before I had set foot in the store, I'd read about the company in
the business press. I knew that it blew away the competition in
terms of employee retention rates and did so by training its employees more extensively than others in the retail industry (more than 10
times the average). Company turnover was barely a third of the industry average of 70 percent for salespeople. You certainly do not
know that you are in a store governed by cutting-edge hiring and
training practices just by walking in and examining its layout and
design. While other companies such as Whole Foods have set-de-
signed a warm and all-encompassing consumer experience for
shoppers, the Container Store décor is bland, minimalist, and fluorescent. But even before I applied, I knew its employees were cut
from a different cloth.

The guiding credo of the Container Store, the psychological un-
derpinning, goes something like this: *The world around us is becoming more disparate, decontextualized, and fragmented, and shopping at
this store will allow you to set up your own fortress of order against the
chaos.* And the store attracts mostly a self-selected crew of believers.
Kim shared with us the man-in-the-desert approach fundamental
to the Container Store operation: A man is lost in the desert until he
finds his way out and wanders into your store. You could give him
some food and water and a telephone to call his family and send

him on his way; that was what most stores did. But the Container Store way was to probe deeper and find out what that man really needed. That man in the desert, that shopper, who comes in looking for a shoe rack may very well need an entire closet redesign. Kim talked of finding the unspoken wants of customers by saying to them, "Let's talk about what you need."

Pete told us about the Skandia shelving that both displays all Container Store merchandise and is one of the company's top-selling products. Part of its allure is the ease with which one can install the shelving onto walls and its durability. Pete jumped up and down on a shelf to show its strength, and then did pull-ups.

Kim said our pay would be 50 to 100 percent higher at the Container Store than at competitors' stores, and that management kept few pieces of information secret—every employee can see the sales numbers for each store. We would have 30 to 40 percent employee discounts. Kim told us that we would know our schedules two to three months ahead of time (instead of the one week typical at other companies) and that the company preferred to start people as part-timers (or "prime-timers"). Kim told us about the "1 = 3 philosophy," which holds that one great person can do the job of three so-so employees. She told us that communication is vital and that every day starts with a huddle.

A 10-minute DVD provided a quick history of the company, starting with its founding in 1978 by Kip Tindell, Garrett Boone, and John Mullen in Dallas. Since then, the store had grown to 36 retail outlets and blossomed into a firm with 20 percent annual sales growth that generated $425 million in 2005. The DVD was peppered with interviews with employees from many stores who showed genuine enthusiasm for their workplace. Unlike other such promotional videos I had seen, their actions and behavior seemed real and unscripted. The DVD made note of the Container Store's repeated selection by *Fortune* as a great place to work; it had been in all six years of the survey and landed in the number-one slot for both 2000 and 2001.

Like other companies where I had applied, the Container Store used an online application, but it asked me to write essays in response to several questions instead of only answering multiple-choice questions whose answers would be scored by a computer. The application seemed to be better tailored to the spirit of the company than other applications I had filled out. The Container Store sold products for organizing, and the application gave you a platform from which to trumpet your own interest in alphabetizing your spices or color-coordinating your running shoe collection. On the application I found room to express myself instead of simply jockeying with an anonymous computer program. I was asked why I wanted to work there and to "tell us more about you." In a final section I was encouraged to "feel free to cut and paste your résumé or any additional information that you feel would allow us to get to know you better." Most companies did not use applications as straightforward as this one but rather prescreened applicants through elaborate testing. Unlike the Container Store, many of the companies where I applied had turned over the rather important task of hiring to a series of algorithms. The context and content of the Container Store group interview and application was in opposition to those of just about all of the other places where I applied.

A FEW WEEKS before I was called in for an interview at the Container Store, I noticed a yawning 25-foot orange "We're Hiring" banner at the Home Depot near my house. Despite the recent climb in the jobless rate, I thought I might have a chance here. It was summertime, so it made sense that Home Depot would hire extra help as homeowners started to do more yard work and kick their home-remodeling projects into gear.

I walked directly to the customer service desk to ask how I might apply. The guy there told me that applications had to be filled out online; I could sit in an office in back or I could go home and fill it out there. So I went home to apply, a process that involved answering more than 100 questions and that took me a half hour. On the application I marked five stores where I wanted to work and the sections of the store I'd prefer: the gardening and paint departments.

After waiting a week and not hearing anything, I drove to one of the five stores to get some face time with a manager. I went to Colma, a suburban town south of San Francisco that sits right off the highway. This Home Depot was designated a "pro" store, one of just a handful worldwide. Store employees there all wore black aprons instead of the typical orange. The workers, and even the shoppers, looked cooler, more relaxed, and in the know. It was the black apron, not the orange, that I wanted to wear, and I was ready to do whatever it took.

An employee a few feet away talked into a cordless phone: "We're going to have to sit down on his attendance; today he said something about having to go to traffic school. It sounded bogus." Then he pushed a button and the phone turned into a loudspeaker; his voice echoed throughout the warehouse as he paged a coworker. "Doug Rogers, pick up line four. Doug."

I gave him a look that said I had a question. I told him I'd applied online and was interested in following up on my application in person. He seemed to like my initiative, smiled warmly, offered a handshake, and introduced himself as Martin, the store manager. He asked why I wanted to work at Home Depot Pro, and I told him it seemed like a well-run outfit. He confided in me the advantages of his store over a nearby Home Depot—something about not having to put on do-it-yourself demonstrations all the time and not having to "stock so many SKUs of carpet." He took down my name and Social Security number and said he would pass the note on to Gary, his human resources manager.

The next day I followed up with Gary, who had already attempted to pull my application off the corporate intranet, without success.

"Alex, did you take the online behavioral test?" he asked.

"Yes, I think so," I said. "I filled out the online application, if that's what you mean."

"Did you answer the ten questions at the beginning?" he said.

"Are those the ten questions that don't really have a right answer?" I asked.

"Yeah," he said. "See, the computer won't allow me to access your file if you've answered these questions incorrectly. That's what I think happened. What you can do is go back online and make sure that you have answered them all. Then call me back. But if you got them wrong, you will have to wait two months before applying again."

I thanked Gary and went back to take a closer look at the questions.

In addition to 90 questions focused on work situations and how I might respond, there were more ambiguous questions with a range of multiple-choice answers. I had tried, in every case, to check off the answer that I thought Home Depot's hiring crew (or at least a computer selection program) would want to see. But as I looked at the questions in a new light, I thought that I might have failed.

1. *Suppose we contacted your most recent supervisors (or teachers). What would they say about how often you make snap decisions?* I was not sure what they were after here. Were they talking about going with your gut? Was this a good thing or a bad thing to do for a Home Depot position? Yes, I imagined, they want someone who is quick on his feet, but impulsive decision making does not

sound like a good thing in an employee. I had checked the box for rarely making snap decisions.

2. *Which describes you best? Calm, collected; team player; conscientious, dependable; enthusiastic?* Okay, I could see here that there couldn't be a "right" answer, because all of those adjectives were positive. I am sometimes calm and collected, other times enthusiastic. But clearly my choice here would be viewed in light of answers I provided on other questions, which, taken together, would shape selection. I went with *conscientious, dependable.*

3. *Other than pens, paper, or other supplies, what is the total worth of all the items and money you have taken from employers in the last 3 years?* My choices included *$0; more than $0 but less than $10; more than $10 but less than $25; more than $25 but less than $100; and $100 or more.* That had to be a trick question, right? Who would actually admit to stealing from an employer? Maybe if I answered that I had not stolen anything, the computer would think I was lying. I went with $0.

4. *How often have you gotten into shoving matches or fistfights at work over the last 3 years?* Again, they had to be kidding. Did people really answer this honestly? I chose *never.*

5. *In the past year, how many times were you late for work (or class)?* This seemed pretty straightforward: I am never late.

6. *Compared to your peers, how often do you lead others?* Now we were getting into tricky territory. I was trying to game the system to get a job, so I was really not sure what I should answer there. Leadership seemed like a good thing to me, but maybe they wanted to hire followers. I really did lack the background to make the right call on that question, but I went with *somewhat more often.*

7. *How often do you rely on others to help you get things done on time?*
Again, murky ground. I needed to show that I was a team player,
but it would clearly be a bad call to say that I don't rely on myself.
Leaning on others is bad, teamwork is good, and self-sufficiency
is a pretty good thing. I went with *occasionally.*

8. *Compared to other employees, how would you perform in a job where
new procedures are constantly being tried out?* I tried to think like
someone from the human resources department: Working somewhere with constant new procedures could be either a great way
to avoid boredom or a big problem. Home Depot wanted to
know how I compared myself to others and how comfortable I
was with change—two big, unrelated ideas crammed into one
small question—making it hard to know which answer to
choose. I decided that if I were in such a changing environment,
I would succeed where others would fail.

Whatever the "right" answers were, I failed to find them. It is
doubtful that any human being ever saw my application; it had
been automatically screened by an algorithm and slotted for dele-
tion. Precious interview time would not be allotted to me. I would
soon fare only a little bit better at Whole Foods Market, the chain
of upscale grocery stores rapidly turning the supermarket industry
on its head—and one of my prime targets. Whole Foods Market
grew from a single natural and organic foods store in Austin,
Texas, in 1980 to a chain of 185 stores by 2006. Since its inception
the company has recognized that the store itself is a key part of
shoppers' experience. Happy, helpful workers—team members, as
they are called—make it possible. In 2006 alone, the firm added
more than 4,500 new jobs, and its workforce already numbered
33,000.

I took several exploratory tours through the local Whole Foods stores. I was not quite Henry David Thoreau hiking through the hills of Concord, but I was acutely focused on the phenomena that surrounded me. I wandered up produce aisles stacked with apples and bananas, and down lanes of vacuum-packed potato chips filed neatly like cordwood. I walked on polished concrete floors, noticed smiles on the faces of the people stocking the shelves, and appreciated the clean lines of stacked cereal boxes.

The markets I explored had created a sense of a town square where you felt okay wasting time, where you might run into someone you knew, and where you felt you were participating in something greater than just grocery shopping. The space inside the store seemed bigger, as if you were outside wandering around a farmer's market, even though you were not. For me, and many people, shopping is a chore, but Whole Foods had addressed part of that problem by reconfiguring the space.

I applied to work for Whole Foods by dropping off a handwritten paper application at a store in San Francisco. A few weeks went by and I heard nothing, so I got in touch with a friend of a friend who worked there, hoping maybe he could help out. I told him I had applied to be a part of the "specialty team" responsible for beer, wine, and cheese.

He emailed back:

I think the best thing to know about Whole Foods is that it's really one of those places where individualism and personality go a long way. It's really up to you how well you match the rest of the team. Most of the time I don't put in recommendations for people I don't know (and they actually frown on us doing so). But I can tell you that the specialty team is a bunch of really cool and dedicated, fun-loving guys and gals. And if you at all have some gourmet food knowledge or interests, along with a good work ethic, you could have a really great shot at it. All the teams in the store are run individually and have their own style and caliber of people they look for. I wish you luck and am hopeful I'll get to work with you.

He suggested I apply online.

At Whole Foods, team members are microspecialists with titles such as *whole body team member, produce sign maker, bodycare team member, bakery specialist,* and (my favorite) *overnight cheese cutter.* For my second Whole Foods application, I needed to choose one job among a dozen possibilities, or at least rank several. In each area, I was sure, I would be able to learn a lot about food. I'd never stood still long enough to gain a strong appreciation for the specific flavors and textures of cuts of beef, the variations in flavor of aged cheeses, and the differences between sea and table salt, so I chose "grocery specialist."

Applying online meant again submitting to a barrage of questions—more than 200—about my work habits. The questions bore some similarities to the questions on the Home Depot application, but not many. The Home Depot questions had addressed a lower common denominator of applicant than did those of Whole Foods. Home Depot seemed to be trying to weed out dishonest, troublesome applicants, whereas Whole Foods was seeking to get to know the applicant's comfort with being a roving team player. The questions were intensely focused and collectively seemed able to tease out the smallest trouble spots in a prospective employee. They seemed to be posed by a brainy psychologist.

The test consisted of statements and a choice of four answers— "strongly disagree," "disagree," "agree," or "strongly agree"—for each statement. Trying to guess which answer would get me invited in for an interview was quite difficult. Statements bobbed and weaved in unpredictable directions and included the basic and the absurd:

You have confidence in yourself. Your stuff is often kind of messy. You like to have exciting fun. It is maddening when the court lets guilty criminals go free. There are some people you really can't stand. You are somewhat of a thrill-seeker. You are always cheerful. You like to stir up excitement when you are bored. It is easy for you to take advantage of others. You are not afraid to tell someone off. You can wait patiently for a long time. Realistically, these days, companies do not expect much loyalty from employees. You deserve to be better off than you are. You like to be alone. Slow people make you impatient. You love to listen to people talk about themselves. Your behavior gets out of control at times. You've done your share of troublemaking. You think about your feelings and try to understand them. You would rather work on a team than by yourself.

The beautiful thing about online applications is that you can apply to work in a city where you don't live. Having had no luck landing a job at Whole Foods in San Francisco, I decided to look for jobs in one of the company's newer, expanding markets: New York City. Whole Foods had already opened three stores in Manhattan, with a fourth soon to follow. The company was starting to alter the city's grocery landscape, and (according to anecdotal evidence) even shape real estate values in the neighborhoods where stores opened. The store in Columbus Circle, all 59,000 subterranean feet of it, was a majestic food emporium. I started looking for a sublet in Manhattan and pulled up the online application. Online I read:

Do you have a passion for healthy food and healthy living? Want to love your job but also need a life? Come work with us at Whole Foods Market, the largest natural and organic foods grocery retailer. Work with great people in a team environment as you learn about natural and organic products from the experts. Our philosophy is to satisfy and delight our customers—and to support team member excellence and happiness.

I applied to join the grocery team as a stocker. If hired, I would "provide excellent customer service, stock and front like a champion, communicate effectively with the team leader and team members, and maintain the break neck [*sic*] pace of the Chelsea Grocery Dept."

Gambling a bit that Whole Foods would come through, I set off for New York City to my new sublet near Columbia University and to what I hoped would be a job through the Thanksgiving and Christmas holidays. After waiting a few days, I called about my application and, after some persistence, managed to arrange an interview for the next day.

I went downtown, walked through the broad doors of the Whole Foods Chelsea store, passed by the produce section, checked in at the customer service desk, and waited for 20 minutes reading *Real Simple*.

The grocery team leader and one of her second-in-command team members took me downstairs into the basement. They put me behind a desk and faced me. They looked quickly at my paperwork and then started the interview.

The team leader was a skinny woman with light brown hair and a decidedly Southern accent. She wanted to know how I organized my pantry, and at first I was not exactly sure what she meant. *Isn't a pantry where you put your washer and dryer?* I thought. *No, a pantry must be where you keep your brooms and mops.* "You know, cabinets, in your kitchen," she said. "We call them pantries down in Tennessee, anyhow." Another question that would make or break me as a candidate. "Well, I don't have much room in my cabinets," I said, as

I summoned up a mental image of my new apartment's minuscule kitchen and its single, bare cabinet. "But in the room that I do have," I stalled, "um, I usually put the stuff, the cans, the cans of soup, that I use the most in the front. And then going back from there, it's the other stuff—crackers, pasta, food that I don't use as much."

"And how do you define good customer service?" she asked.

"It means never saying no to the customer; it means bending over backward to make the customer feel welcome and doing whatever you can to help them out," I said.

"You got it! Rock on!" she said.

The interview seemed to go well, though I could tell the picture I presented confused the two. I'd told them that I was in graduate school, but they wanted to know if I had some additional means of income. I came across as good at customer service, but they got hung up on the fact that I didn't have any directly related experience. "You have never stocked shelves, and that's a problem," the team leader said. At the end of the interview, she said she would call me right away to set a follow-up interview with her boss.

In New York for more than a month, I never got a call back from Whole Foods. I came to wonder if I had failed Whole Foods' online exam, whether the psychological test had ruled me out. Thinking of the Whole Foods workers I knew and had observed, I wondered whether the test, perhaps a proprietary tool, might be at the root of the company's hiring of workers who struck me as individualists—or at least people who outwardly displayed more individuality than workers at places such as Home Depot. But months later I encountered a virtually identical test when I was applying to work as a noncommissioned salesperson at consumer electronics retailer Best Buy. With my background and relationship to work, it was not surprising that I failed these prescreening tests.

INTO THE DATA STREAM

The first job I had was when I was in high school, as a member of a small construction crew. Initially my role was chiefly to demolish things such as lath-and-plaster walls, buy doughnuts for the team, and run errands, but over a few summers I gained some carpenter's skills. Odd jobs continued through college: I worked as an assistant to a professor of underwater archeology; I cooked for 150 scientists at a high-altitude biology laboratory in Colorado; I proofread a 20-volume legal series on workers' compensation. Long before I had a real job, I had developed an unusual relationship with work. The workplace had been an area of endless curiosity for me, and perhaps because of this, after college I followed my wide-ranging interests into journalism.

In my last year of college, I took a test called the Birkman Method, designed in the 1940s by Roger W. Birkman, a World War II pilot who worked with a group of scientists at the University of Texas to survey psychological instruments for Air Force pilot selection. By the time I used this assessment tool, more than a million people had also taken it. This number was important because the way my answers were analyzed relied, in part, on the answers of previous test takers. Through a process of regression and factor analysis, the Birkman test identifies a person's interpersonal style, underlying motivations, expectations, and stress behavior. The test sought to identify my strengths, weaknesses, and general aptitudes for different kinds of work by repeatedly asking me to select between options, such as whether I would prefer to work as a farmer or as a dentist or to sell flowers or cars.

When my test results came back, I read them over and filed them away, feeling as if the report didn't really tell me anything I didn't already know and didn't help me to better shape a career. The advice felt like the one-size-fits-all anodyne prose you read in horoscopes and fortune cookies—ideas you can always apply to yourself: *You will encounter periods of financial difficulty; stay frugal. Friends are particularly important at this time; keep them near.*

But now, years later, as I sought work on the front lines and found myself taking more and more online tests, I reexamined the Birkman results and could see a clear theme. The section of the report directed to my potential employers advised them to:

- Provide nonconfining activities (freedom)
- Make sure assignments involve change and variety, but don't overload him with simultaneous tasks
- Keep close controls to a minimum and avoid routine schedules
- Allow changes to be a matter of choice where possible
- Avoid giving assignments of an immediate nature

The report further pointed out some of my character traits:

- Finds it hard to adjust to rules and procedures that are not flexible
- Is realistic and restrained, but only within a framework that permits and encourages freedom of expression
- Avoids methods and procedures that do not involve novelty, change, and spontaneous action
- Needs the stimulation of constant change and a sense of adventure

Though intuitively I already knew it to be so, the test clearly showed that I was not an ideal hire for the front lines, taking orders from a sequence of managers and supervisors. Presumably, the application tests I was now taking online also showed that I was not much of a team player and was unlikely to blossom in the environments where I was applying to work. In every case I had answered in ways that I thought would be more likely to get me hired, but as I tried to game the tests at Whole Foods, Home Depot, and elsewhere, it appeared my true disposition to work remained visible.

When I was asked to agree or disagree with statements such as "You like to be in the middle of a big crowd" and "It's fun to go out to events with big crowds," I agreed (even though I really do not). When asked whether I "like to talk a lot," "love to be with people," and "chat with people [I] don't know," I agreed as well. These are things I do not really like but traits that I deemed I *should* like if I wanted to be hired. In a similar vein, I disagreed that I "do not like small talk," that "people who talk all the time are annoying," that I "could not deal with difficult people all day," and that I "would rather not get involved in other people's problems." Answering in ways that I thought would make me appear to be an ideal front-line employee, I wondered just how the tests were calling my bluff.

The tests I was finding online traced their history to personality tests such as the 1919 Woodworth Personal Data Sheet, designed to help the Army screen out recruits who might be susceptible to shell shock, and subsequent personality tests such as the Thematic Apperception Test and the Minnesota Multiphasic Personality Inventory. These rudimentary placement tests were based on the recognition that people differ in ways that have measurable effects on how well they adjust to and perform in different jobs. The tests aggregate data to show that individual differences in ability and personality have significant implications for occupational placement, success, and adjustment. The chief difference between the online tests I was taking and the test I had taken in college is that people taking tests to get a job are strongly motivated to defeat the test to win the job, and job tests are built to withstand this challenge.

Like most workers applying for hourly-wage jobs, I had little idea what was going on behind the scenes. I later discovered that the applications used by Best Buy and Whole Foods were both created by a company called Unicru, an Oregon-based firm that helps companies select workers. Unicru is no small player in this burgeoning field: It processed more than 2.6 million employment applications in 2000 and 14.6 million applications in 2005; that same year, it helped 10 of the top 20 U.S. retailers and scores of other companies to hire more than 1.2 million applicants.

Unicru was launched in 1987 and the first scientist hired was an MBA-Ph.D. design modeling statistician named David Scarborough. Together with a team of economists, lawyers, and organizational psychologists, Scarborough and his statisticians crafted the questions for the tests I had taken. When I called to ask him about these tests, Scarborough explained that each question, though it might not appear so, is tied directly to a job and designed to predict the success of the applicant in that job. He referred to the applications not as tests but as employment questionnaires.

The questions that seemed out of context to me, for example— "You change from feeling happy to sad without any reason"—each had a distinct purpose. The answer to each question "provides a psychological measurement that correlates with better performance on the job," Scarborough told me.

The tests also ask similar questions multiple times so that, taken together, the answers yield a score for a certain trait. For a basic hourly-wage retail job, five or six scores are often captured, such as patience, confidence, optimism, happiness, and sociability. "You can calculate a 'patience' score for an individual because you have tested many, many people and you know how people answer that same set of questions, so you know how that person compares to all those other people who have taken the same test," Scarborough told me. This is the essence of these tests, to compare one to many.

Though I'd thought I was gaming the system, organizational psychologists call this posturing "favorable self-presentation," something that, to some extent, all job seekers practice. Favorable self-presentation is part of putting on a good face and getting a job, but it's also something that modern employment tests are designed to detect, build controls for, assign a score to, and use to identify anomalies like me. In and of itself, favorable self-presentation can be a predictor of job success among populations such as salespeople. Unicru plots a favorable self-presentation index on a distribution curve and identifies break points on that graph: If a test taker presents too favorably on one of these distributions, he or she is essentially lying, in the view of the test. If you agree, say, that "you have never gotten angry at anyone," the test assumes that you are not being truthful. If a test taker answers a series of questions in an unexpected way, the probability of lying increases.

After I took the tests for Whole Foods and Best Buy, the hiring manager probably received an email summarizing my application that contained enough information to enable an employment decision on the spot. Because I was trying to game the system, my favorable self-presentation index score was abnormally high, which probably kept me from getting an interview, or later precluded me from being hired.

In high-turnover sectors of the marketplace, screening, no matter how it is executed, is critical. The tests showed me that companies go to great lengths to screen, and that a less-than-ideal or low-quality hire can adversely affect future applicants. Not only are applicant data tracked but also workers' on-the-job performance is correlated to the ways in which they answered the original questions. In other words, it is believed that correlations observed among current and former workers will also be observed in the population of future workers. When an employee is fired for poor attendance, original test scores are linked so that the systems can try to identify statistical markers of job success for new applicants. Unlike paper-based systems, the online application systems can yield so much data that the only way to analyze them is through data mining and using artificial intelligence techniques to draw conclusions and recognize patterns. The systems get smarter over time and constantly incorporate data from workplace databases such as payroll and customer-service ratings.

"When an applicant walks in and sits down in front of the computer, we can process that incoming data stream statistically and make an actuarial estimate of their likely job success, and then feed that information back to the hiring manager, who can then make a statistically informed hiring decision," said Scarborough. "That is the principal advantage of these online criterion-valid selection tools."

The way I had been thinking about the tests was completely wrong. I imagined that the employer was mostly seeking to weed out bad apples, but it's not just "good worker" versus "bad worker" that they look for. They're searching for a select menu of traits they have identified and can change as needed. I had been under the false impression that there were people who liked to make small talk, never solved disputes with fistfights, and never stole from their employers. But employers have to hire from real populations, not imaginary ones. Unicru says that by using its tests, firms see an average decrease of 10 to 30 percent in employee turnover and a more than 50 percent reduction in hiring time. The hope is that the system will allow employers to clone their best, most reliable people. "When we design a questionnaire, we have to not only be aware of the general characteristics of good salespeople that tend to be universal, but we also have to be aware of the sales environment in which they will be working. So selling a car is very different from selling clothing, which is very different from selling tacos. A lot of the questionnaires reflect the different environment. The job content itself drives the test content," Scarborough told me.

Scarborough sees what he calls "a service industry paradox," in which the least-valued employee population has the largest effect on the survival of a service company. Though profitability depends on the efficacy of the front-line employee, few companies pay attention to this. "Churn and burn of hourly workers is an outdated concept," he said.

You need a core of believers staffing the front lines, and the idea behind Unicru-style tests is that before you even worry about studying a particular worker's on-the-job habits, you need to make sure he or she is someone you want to have on staff. You can optimize the worker for the job long before he or she starts working and maximize the efficiency of an organization by ensuring that each member fits. The new techniques, it was clear, are able to select workers with brutal efficiency, but no doubt certain workers would find getting work much harder. The tests are so accurate that they seem almost to violate one's privacy. "It is not the job of the machine to hire people—it is the hiring manager's job. So we provide a decision-support service, not a decision maker," said Scarborough.

In my case, the decisions seemed to be going against me. The computer software, like an X-ray, was looking right through my self-created job-applicant persona. Despite my efforts, my individualist, nonjoiner self was apparent, which meant that I was regularly failing the tests. It began to seem that I might not be able to join the front lines after all. Until I filled out the Container Store's test and was called in for a group interview, I wondered whether my undercover project would even be possible.

THIS IS WHAT WE DO

About halfway through the Container Store interview, Pete assigned us a basic exercise: We were to walk around the store and pick out a few items we wanted to share. I picked a container with a hinging, sealable top to store dry dog food. I also picked a tubular document holder that would allow me to buttress my story about being in school. (Though I used my real name, I said I was a graduate student with very little work experience.)

After a break we went around the room sharing why we had picked each item, again starting with me. My comments were perfunctory and I neglected to mention that I already used such a dog food dispenser and that I had built a mechanism to stow the container under a cupboard. I blew it, while other people nailed the exercise. Most went for big, splashy items, but Lily, the craftswoman sitting next to me, chose just two pieces: a small spring-loaded plastic container for storing quarters and a slice-of-bread-with-crust-shaped Tupperware container for holding sandwiches. She already owned and used each item—one held her parking meter change and the other protected her sandwiches. She spoke about the things naturally and with an understated passion. Ricky, a disheveled recent college graduate with long hair and baggy pants, brought back a stainless-steel gumball-style dispenser that he told us would hold the cereal he ate day and night. He was less convincing. Mike brought back the more pedestrian: a suitcase with wheels and a magnetic calendar. Elizabeth spread her selections in front of her chair: a red neoprene wine bottle holder she intended to use to tote wine on picnics, an orange computer case to carry her laptop to class, and an ice-cube holder for her fridge.

Cynthia was a Texan with a completely bald head (part of her plan to clean up, move to California, and get organized). "I was sick of the clutter, so I shaved my head too," she told us. She hauled back a hefty butcher-block island that she said was the last piece she needed to complete a kitchen. I might not have gone far enough, but she had gone too far. Joyce shared a handful of small plastic multicolored translucent boxes she hoped to use to separate her earrings. Jerome described himself as a mad collector who had moved from accumulating matches to collecting shot glasses. He now collected computer games and showed us a basic black case he would use to organize his budding collection. Andrea held up some square black frames she would use to display album covers on her apartment walls.

Once everyone had spoken and Kim had thanked us for "what we had brought to today's circle," Pete piped up. "What we just did is what we do," he said. He let his words hang for a second. What we had just *done*, selling each other by sharing our own passions for these items, was what we would *do* as employees of the Container Store. Some people had invoked their true passion, others had not.

Instead of following a tight script, our interview had offered a prolonged exercise in actual doing. There were no hypotheticals here; we were in the moment: 10 individuals sitting around a virtual campfire sharing our own ways of approaching modern life. The context of the interview had allowed for a basic, spontaneous sales audition by each one of us as we were encouraged to forget what we were doing and be ourselves. The traditional interview had been ditched in favor of a radical overhaul.

What we just did is what we do. It was a simple statement, but Pete had pointed out what made this interview different from others. The Container Store fills its ranks with just the kind of people who would, without prodding, buy what the store sells because they love the stuff. Pete mentioned that many employees found working there to be a veritable support group for organizing. It was a ridiculously basic idea: If you wanted to find people who could sell by sharing, who better to sell than people already passionate about the items for sale? While some niche stores do this as a matter of habit, it's rare to see it in a large organization.

Pete and Kim said we should hear back from the company soon. I went around the corner to eat lunch and collect my thoughts. Compared to the places I had interviewed so far, I left the Container Store with the best impression yet. The Container Store pulled in an advanced talent pool from which it could then select the best candidates.

I visualized the circle of faces in our meeting and tried to eliminate eight of the 10 from consideration. Who were the two I would hire if I were Pete and Kim? This was a group of articulate and experienced applicants. If the hiring were up to me, I would hire those with passion. Deciding who not to hire was easy: First on the cutting block were the quiet shot glass collector and me. But choosing among the others was harder. I decided I would hire Lily the craftswoman and Elizabeth the Ph.D. candidate because they exemplified what the Container Store was looking for.

The group interview did an interesting thing: It showed you just who the first round of cuts were. You actually got to see your competition up close. And when I mentally lined up the Gap crew of 10 I had been with two days before alongside the 10 at the Container Store, there was no comparison. Surely they could afford to be more picky at the Container Store; they needed to hire a couple of people, while the group interview at Gap would cut out only five of the 10 applicants. (In 2005, the Container Store received 32,000 applications, added just 117 jobs, and had a total workforce of just 3,000, whereas Gap's workforce was more than 150,000.) They might both be selling stuff, but the Container Store and Gap pull their stock of employees from completely different places.

I might have been invited to the Container Store group interview because I was enthusiastic and forthcoming on my application, but in the interview I failed by not being myself, not true to the Container Store way. And during the pivotal exercise, I choked. Instead of cruising around the store and identifying products I was passionate about, I casually grabbed a plastic dog food holder and told the group that it would provide my dog with fresher food. I had worried that showing too much genuine enthusiasm would make me come across as a fake, but by not being myself, I was pretty sure I had failed the test. Faking a persona is something that computers and human interviewers alike can identify, and both the online tests and group interviews could probe and decipher who I was in a way that these employers had deemed critical. Online and offline approaches were both incisive, if invasive, but both were able to figure out my makeup and relevance to their needs.

It was a bummer, but not a major surprise, when a week after the interview at the Container Store I received a brief email. It read simply:

Hello, Alex: Thank you for your interest in employment opportunities with The Container Store. We enjoyed meeting you recently at our group interview and hope you left with the same level of enthusiasm that we all share for our company. We carefully considered your potential employment with our company, and unfortunately, we are unable to consider you further for a position. . . . We look forward to seeing you again as a customer at The Container Store!

I had to concede that the system had worked. They had not found in me the necessary passion that they needed, and they had weeded me out. But Enterprise Rent-A-Car wanted me.

THREE

TWO TRUTHS AND ONE LIE

If you were to look at a map of the San Francisco Bay Area with the aim of choosing one of its least pleasant corners, San Leandro would be a good choice: It is largely a city of industry, it has a wide freeway that divides it in half, it is in the direct flight path of a major airport, and it sports a handful of inelegant strip malls. Early on a Monday morning I ventured there to the local headquarters of Enterprise Rent-A-Car. If you are selected to work at Enterprise in the Bay Area, as I was, this is where your career begins.

Enterprise's group headquarters administrative office, GPBR 2399, is a dull, rectangular box set along an industrial parkway not far from the highway. Once I was inside, I joined a dozen class-mates, each sitting behind a computer as we waited for our teacher. The room was basic, with venetian blinds pulled shut against the morning sun and, on one side of the room, a green counter equipped with active branch computers. The seats we chose became our regular spots for the next week, so I ended up in the back row where I would have a good view of the class. Looking around the room, I saw my fellow trainees as molten steel ready to be poured into molds. In just two weeks, we would be sprung from these molds and installed in the vast Enterprise machine.

If some companies, such as the Container Store, Home Depot, and Whole Foods, take great pains to bring in only those employees with the best cultural fit, other companies focus on hiring applicants who exhibit enough potential that they might be molded to fit the culture through intensive training. Enterprise seemed to be such a place, committed to bringing its new charges into a culture of ambition and managerial aspiration. Because Enterprise would begin with an in-depth training course, something rarely found in similar front-line workplaces, I would have a chance to see how training could be used both to teach new workers skills in a dedicated teaching environment and to indoctrinate this new staff, to build new team members out of an unaffiliated group.

Soon our trainer arrived. She was Zoë, a no-nonsense woman in her early thirties with long brown hair tied in a smart bun. From the moment she arrived to command our attention her focus never wandered, despite the fact that she was close to nine months pregnant and commuted more than an hour each way to work. Immediately she gave us the impression that she knew her material thoroughly. We had been selected from a larger pool of applicants, so Zoë immediately gave us a groupwide pat on the back and told us that in the Bay Area a scant 4 percent of those interviewed at Enterprise are hired. (Later, one of my more skeptical classmates would tabulate that 400 people would have had to have been interviewed to leave the 12 of us for hiring. He found the ratio dubious.) "Someone," she told us, "saw an area manager in each of you."

Zoë began our training by presenting a PowerPoint slide show that detailed the history and mission of Enterprise. Started humbly in 1957 by Jack Taylor, Enterprise was named after the aircraft carrier U.S.S. *Enterprise* and was still privately owned and run by his son, Andy. Zoë stood in front of us and an animated slide in which an arrow slowly circled among the three interrelated words that comprised the Enterprise equation: *Customers* ⟶ *Employees* ⟶ *Profits*. The arrow also crossed over Zoë's forehead during each revolution. Those three words might have been all we needed to know.

Following Zoë's orders, we paired up and learned one another's biographies. We were an ethnically diverse mix and included an African-American woman, several white men, a Filipino-American woman, two Asian-American men, and a Jordanian émigré. As management trainees, or MTs, we were the company's freshman class. We would be paid by the hour and would not take part in corporate profit sharing. If we completed this mandatory first step, we could begin our ascent upward toward the levels of management assistant, branch manager, area manager, and beyond—at a company that says it promotes exclusively from within. Though my fellow classmates might have been moldable metal, I was less pliable. The interview process had made me cynical from the start: There seemed something cultlike and more demanding of sacrifice at Enterprise than at other front-line workplaces.

I BECAME INTERESTED in working at Enterprise Rent-A-Car after a trip to Canada. I'd rented cars from Enterprise before; it was a company that seemed vaguely family-run, with every branch attended by an abundance of young people all wearing pressed white shirts, smiling a lot, and jumping back and forth from their computer terminals to the printer. The crew in Canada arranged to reduce a one-way drop-off fee I had to pay after driving from the British Columbia Interior. Airport locations are not a focus for Enterprise, so when I dropped off my car in Vancouver the branch was a few miles from Vancouver International. Like other branches, this one was staffed by eager young guys who looked like they had just graduated from college. I was running late for my plane, so the hyperactive guy checking me in offered to drive me to the terminal. I asked him what made Enterprise different. "Our customer service, I guess?" he said. "And we try harder!" he said ironically.

As an Enterprise customer, I easily picked up on an overarching energy that seemed to govern workers' activities. Employees, regardless of rank, were not above working directly with customers and doing everything to ensure a positive experience. I couldn't see how this ethic was instilled in workers, but I was interested in becoming part of the company to find out.

The Enterprise website described in detail the entry-level job I was applying for: "As a Management Trainee at Enterprise, you'll learn to run a profit center, manage people, and grow your own fast-paced business. You'll enjoy big earning potential in a hurry, with performance-based promotion that many MBAs would envy. Plus you'll find great opportunities, fun people, and a $6 billion company." The job seemed different from others I had seen: a genuine training opportunity that would provide skills you could export to your next job or use to climb within the company.

Each company has a different strategy to attract employees. Starbucks dangles the prospect of health insurance for workers who put in more than 20 hours on average a week. Enterprise promises that you will acquire a "virtual MBA." For recent college graduates, the chance to gain a firm toehold on the lower rungs of a corporate ladder is no doubt more attractive than renting out cars as hourly employees, though that is chiefly what the job entails.

I was soon in application mode, answering a series of questions that had "no right or wrong responses." In the "work styles questionnaire," I answered questions about my preferred or typical work behavior. I used a drop-down menu to select from five options: *strongly agree, agree, unsure, disagree,* and *strongly disagree.* The instructions said to "not give a response because you think it is the right thing to say" and cautioned that there are "certain checks built into the questionnaire to give us an indication of how honest you have been."

The more than 60 questions were a meditation on the postmillennial workplace:

I seek variety in all things I do. I stick with tasks until they are completed. I like to be highly active. I always give people my full attention. I tend to conceal my feelings. I like repetitive work. I enjoy making a sale. I like to keep busy. I am less ambitious than other people. I rarely display my emotions. I am not always very considerate to other people. I rarely change how I act in different situations. I enjoy work the most when there is a great deal to do. I set high goals for myself. I never feel envious of other people. I have never engaged in gossip. Routine bores me. I never annoy my colleagues. I enjoy selling ideas to clients. I behave differently depending on who is with me. I am not particularly ambitious. People know how I'm feeling. I am very supportive in times of need. I display my emotions openly. I like to work in one place. I dislike having too much to do. I set targets which are easily achievable. Selling is not one of my strong points.

After failing other online tests, I was surprised and relieved to get an email inviting me to the local headquarters of Enterprise for my first interview. I threw on a blue sport coat and a pair of slacks and drove to an office park that doubled as a depot where Enterprise sold used cars. I sat in a soulless waiting room decorated with three posters, all variations of ocean waves hitting a red-and-white-striped lighthouse on what looked like the coast of Newfoundland. After I had waited 20 minutes, the recruiter escorted me to her office. She was in her mid-forties, had long brown hair, and wore a suit. She fired off a few questions, took copious notes, and told me that I had more selling experience than I might have thought. She also warned me of three things I would not like: long hours, "brutal clients," and that "it's not a glamorous job." She explained my pay structure and said that in a year or so, I would be able to get a bonus and "write my own paycheck." (I was told that I would make about $36,000 per year, but this number was misleading: It was not a salary but hourly pay calculated with de facto overtime hours.)

I did a good enough job at the interview for her to set up another one with the woman who would be my area manager. But I was an anomaly, or at least I should have been. I was not a recent college graduate (I'd graduated a decade before), and according to the résumé I supplied, I had made a living as a construction helper and as a waiter. But though I might not have been a standard Enterprise applicant, this did not appear to trip any alarms.

For my second interview I went directly to an Enterprise branch. I sat in the waiting room and flipped through a well-worn copy of *Exceeding Expectations,* a book about the company, and learned that renting cars was a new service in the 1950s and that Enterprise was a pioneer in the field. Then Yvette, the area manager, showed me to a bare back room. She sat behind a dark wood-veneered desk and asked me to sell her something.

"Like what?" I asked her.

"Sell me your watch!" she said.

I stared at my black Casio. "This watch is great. I have one myself," I said to her. "I use it every day. Are you a runner? Well, then this is the watch for you. It has a stopwatch that works really well. And I personally use it a lot to wake up in the morning. I don't even need an alarm clock! It's great for traveling too. It has not one but three alarms and even a snooze button. Try one today; I can offer you a thirty-day trial."

"Great," she said. "Sold!"

For my third, and last, interview I again reported to the regional headquarters, this time to meet with Graciela, a slim, flashily dressed woman in her late thirties who, as regional rental manager, was second in command of the North Bay, or AA, region. She greeted me and walked me to her spacious second-floor office that looked out on a marsh. Inside, sitting in a chair alongside her desk, was Bert, a guy with curly brown hair who was a few years younger than me and who would be my manager if I were hired. We exchanged hellos and then got down to business.

The interview was hard-hitting enough that I figured they would see right through my charade. But their questions showed that they were mostly interested in how ambitious and how ready to sell things I was. Was I a leader? Would I be able to handle working 60-plus hours a week? What were some examples I could share with them of being competitive? I'd competed as a cyclist and runner but decided that those sports were too much about individual endurance, not teamwork, so I instead described participation in group sports such as soccer to demonstrate my leadership skills and raw competitive spirit. At one point toward the end, the manager motioned to the regional leader and indicated that she had been with the company just seven years and had handily and steadily ascended the ranks. "She is doing awesome financially," he said as she smiled. "She's pretty much set, and in just seven years." I nodded in agreement.

The list of promises I heard during the recruiting process seemed hard to believe. I quickly learned that the passion among those who interviewed me was not about the corporate asset, renting cars, or a craft or skill one would learn, but about the career itself, its inherent financial rewards and its limitless potential for growth. I was dubious from the outset but eager to see how incentives would be used to motivate us.

DURING ORIENTATION I learned the following about my classmates: Ted was a 25-year-old who spoke in the drawl of his native
Maine and said he was sequentially reading all of Graham Swift's
novels. Well dressed and well organized, he inserted several dozen
color-coded sticker flags into his training binder over the course of
the week. Akiko, 23, sat next to Ted and was reading Gabriel
García Márquez's *Love in the Time of Cholera*. Yolanda said she
could only read books and go to movies with happy endings. She
was reading a book called *The Complete Idiot's Guide to Creative Vi-
sualization* and during breaks listened to a CD that accompanied
the book. She went to bed early every night. Gordon was six-foot-
three and though heavyset, was more wide and flat than fat. He
had just graduated from Sacramento State, where he worked part
time at a pharmacy. Though Linda had worked at a branch for
more than six months, she had not yet been to training. She became
my secret weapon, telling me a second time how to do everything.
Leah was still in college and wore pants she bought at Target that
she hemmed with straight pins.

To break the ice, we played a game called "Two Truths and One
Lie," where we each took a piece of paper and wrote down two true
things about ourselves and then one untruth. The group then voted
on which statement was a lie. The winner gained the most points
by deceiving the most people. The exercise had tricky undertones:
One woman wrote that she had majored in both chemistry and biology, which seemed a stretch but apparently was not. Another
timid woman wrote that she was a "loud sorority girl," and that did
not seem right. One classmate sitting on my left, who had alluded
to a prior career as an Oakland police officer, wrote that he liked to
cook, had been a high school football star, and had shot four guys in
the leg. We all took his word for the shootings and incorrectly voted
against his football stardom. With an entirely manufactured background, I produced three bland truths for the group.

Every one of us was dressed in "conservative, professional business attire," which meant suits for the men and suitlike outfits for the women, the uniforms specified in the welcome letters sent to us. We seven men wore suits that were off-the-rack and cheaply woven. As time went on, we would wear those suits in places such as gas stations and Taco Bells where we would stand out as overdressed, and we would also wash cars while we were wearing them. But suits set us apart from the polo shirt–clad competition at Avis and Hertz and arguably defined us as businesspeople, not simply service people or hourly workers (which we really were). I wore a suit I bought on the eve of college graduation; it still fit but was quite tight. We were told that by the time we were branch managers, we would be expected to own five suits and that we were to wear only white dress shirts, except on Fridays, when baby blue was allowed. According to the official dress code doublespeak, "radical departures from conventional dress or personal grooming are not permitted" and "although extremes of any kind should be avoided . . . current styles are not discouraged, nor is individualism."

In class we learned Enterprise's founding values—"The Values That Define Us and Drive Us"—which included "Our brand is the most valuable thing we own." Zoë asked us what we thought *brand* meant. One student ventured that a brand is an image we have in our mind. Zoë asked us to imagine that we had arrived in a foreign country where we didn't speak the language. There, we saw a red box with a yellow m inside of it. "What does that symbol mean?" she asked. It's the brand of McDonald's, we all told her in unison, and she told us that this was branding. She asked us to consider the images associated with the Ford Explorer and the *Exxon Valdez,* and to ponder the public-relations nightmare when an unattached finger was found in a bowl of chili at a Wendy's restaurant. She explained the perils of negative branding: Small mistakes and em-

ployee shortcuts can harm a brand, she said. Sending off a car
without an oil change can come back to haunt us.

After an information-packed morning, we went to lunch at an
Applebee's restaurant tucked next to a highway overpass. The pre-
dominantly male side of the table bonded over surf-and-turf plat-
ters and virgin piña coladas. I sat at the other end with my female
coworkers. Each spoke of disapproving parents who had expressed
concern about their job choice, some version of "You didn't go to
college to start working at a rental car company." "You know, they
just don't get it," Akiko said. My coworkers viewed their job as a
deviation from the norm, but I was still not sure whose side I was
on, that of the concerned parent or of the dismissive kid. Enterprise
clearly values college graduates and has figured out how to attract
them in a big way. In fact, having hired 7,000 in 2006, Enterprise
became one of the largest recruiters of college kids in the United
States. But it was early yet in my Enterprise experience, too early to
reach any conclusions.

After lunch we piled back into the 15-seat white van we had
shuttled over in, driven by an employee from Enterprise's vanpool
division. As we drove back to headquarters and our classroom, the
four of us crammed into the back row discussed what we were
going to do with our first paychecks (pay off our credit card bills). I
lost track of what direction we were driving but sensed that we
might have been driving in circles. And in fact we were. Zoë had
spotted a car on the side of the highway and was certain it had an
Enterprise "e" sticker on its rear bumper. Employees who stop to
offer customer assistance on the roadside are eligible for $100 from
the company. Zoë decided that stopping and helping would be a
great learning opportunity, a way to put in practice what she was
teaching us. So we wound our way through the pretzel-shaped on-
and off-ramps and approached the ailing customer.

Our van slid in behind a blue Dodge Neon and three students disembarked. The customer had curly black hair combed over his balding head, was sweating, and looked concerned. He had a flat tire and had been waiting for more than an hour for assistance, only to be met by a white van full of mostly 20-year-olds in ill-fitting business clothes, looking like a group of Mormons on a road trip. Sitting in the rear of a van protected only by a sheet-metal bumper along the side of U.S. 880, one of the nation's busiest highways, as I was, seemed unwise. I gazed through the rear window as battalions of 18-wheelers bore down on us, and I speculated about the inevitable collision and subsequent postmortem insurance battles between our families and Enterprise. Gordon, Nate, and Dennis, who were all, like me, wearing crisp white button-down shirts, managed to fix the flat and send the customer on his way. Like a kayaker eddying into a river, he aimed his small white car into the flow of traffic, pulled out, and waved thanks to all of us.

The risk we had experienced had its reward, pedagogically speaking. That afternoon, Zoë turned the highway stop into a training session on the value of customer service at Enterprise and the notion of building a customer for life. It was a rare moment of a class lesson in action: Instead of talking about real-life situations and role-playing, we'd actually done something. In general, though, role-playing was a staple of training at Enterprise, as elsewhere. We each had a chance to play the role of customer and employee in a variety of situations. One day we were boisterous customers trying our best to fluster the staff; another day we were employees trying to sign up customers for insurance coverage.

One of the chief subjects we focused on was how to properly fill out contracts with customers. This was all fairly straightforward, save for the part in which we offered the customer three choices for insurance coverage: a basic damage waiver starting at $8.99 per day, a supposedly more thorough supplemental liability protection for $11.99 a day, and a personal accident insurance for three to seven dollars a day. A good deal of our time in class was spent learning the nuances of signing customers up for this coverage, and our training included learning how to counter customers' many objections. We learned tools and proper responses to criticism. "Sales 101," said Zoë, "means starting with a question." She said that "How do you plan to cover this vehicle?" was a good one to start with.

During our five days of official training, each learning module was tied directly to the liability and profit it reflected. Zoë said that there were low margins on the insurance products, and that Enterprise offers them only as an extension of its customer service. But this was extremely hard to believe, given the amount of time we spent learning about it. (According to one industry analyst, incremental revenue, such as that from insurance and rental of child car seats, accounts for a quarter of total revenues in the rental car industry.) Although Zoë told us that the company prides itself on being "not in the rental-car business but in the customer-service business," the customer-service section of the training binder was just 10 pages, while the section on selling insurance was 73 pages— the longest section in the book. Though nobody at Enterprise said as much, it was quite clear that we were chiefly insurance salespeople.

We learned a wealth of excuses that customers would give us as to why they didn't need to take out our insurance: *My credit card covers me; my insurance covers me; you're getting a commission; I'm rich and I don't need it.* One excuse we were told we would hear was that people would not want insurance because their religious beliefs don't allow gambling; some religions (such as Jehovah's Witness) interpret insurance to be a form of gambling. Others would tell us that they simply don't need insurance because, they would say, "The Lord Jesus Christ will protect me." If someone were to invoke the powers of a deity, we were not to try to dissuade them but were encouraged to find creative ways to break through even that excuse. When I role-played a customer in class, I told Yolanda, the serious young woman with dyed-red cornrows, that I did not need her insurance because God would be watching my back. "God is also watching over me," she said, without missing a beat. "But he would want me to get insurance because we never know his plans."

Zoë emphasized the importance of selling insurance. "Look," she said, "if they don't want coverage, you are going to want to paint a picture for them: 'Okay, so you are fiddling with the radio dial when some 16-year-old blasts through the stoplight and T-bones that brand-new Nissan Maxima that you've just rented from us. You've got whiplash and the total cost of repair exceeds $5,000. You decided against the twenty-dollar-a-day coverage we offer. So now what's your game plan, guy?' "

After class we were sent to the Oakland Airport Hilton, where we would stay for the week. We were told that this living arrangement had been provided so that we could avoid a daily commute, and we were given $60 to cover our meals during the week. It seemed clear to me that having us all stay in one place would also serve to reinforce our new training; if we did not go home at night to our friends and normal lives, we would be less likely to question the information we were taking in each day. After 5 PM we all motored over to the hotel and checked in, and then found out who our roommates would be. The airport hotel had several two-story buildings and a sports bar that was home to die-hard Oakland Raiders fans. In the early evening, about half our group reconvened in the sports bar to work on the 25 questions that Zoë had sent us home with, such as "What does *VIN* stand for?" and "What is embezzlement?" All the answers were easily found in our training binders. The group was eager, and it was exciting to see people so fired up at the start of their careers. We ordered drinks as we did our homework. Some peeled off for their rooms, a handful of guys played poker, and still others drank more and more into the evening. After a few drinks, I went out for some dinner and then back to my room.

My roommate was Dennis, the one guy who might have been near my age and who had mentioned during class that he had previously worked as a police officer making six figures. It was still unclear why he would want to start at this low-paying job, where we would make well under $40,000 a year. I'd brought the 1940s bestseller *How to Win Friends and Influence People,* which I read in our room as I awaited his return. Like Ishmael waiting for Queequeg at the Spouter Inn in *Moby-Dick,* I faced an intimate lodging arrangement with a new workmate. Unlike Ishmael, though, I would not be shipping out on the high seas to hunt whales; I would be renting vehicles to customers. At midnight Dennis returned victoriously from the bar, where he had been drinking heavily with Amir, the Jordanian émigré in our class. "Dude, that guy Amir can drink!" said Dennis. "Damn, dude—I am wasted. We drank Long Islands and Long Beaches, and then we washed it all down with beer. I guess that's what they do where he is from. Dude, I am wasted!"

Dennis turned on the TV, weaved toward his bed, pulled back the sheets, and passed out face-down in his clothes, clutching the remote control. I kept reading for a while in bed as Dennis's snoring moved into lower octaves, resonating and shaking the room. As the snoring got louder, I inserted a pair of earplugs that I had fortuitously packed, but they proved worthless. Next I tried listening to music to drown out the sound, but I found it hard to sleep with Nirvana thumping in my headphones.

At two in the morning I lay awake in bed. My roommate's snoring was so loud that I could not sleep. My roommate had, rather incongruously, kept the peace in the town in which we now lay in an airless hotel room. Enterprise did not really know any more about my roommate than they knew about me. I was sharing a room with a mysterious stranger. I sat up in bed, head propped on a pillow, and watched an infomercial about a scheme whose participants would all become wildly rich. It was classic, full of images of wealthy, well-dressed individuals driving nice cars and parking them on lush pastoral estates. There was something that rang true here and made me think of Enterprise: They were promising us all something that we could not all possibly attain. Some of us would advance and others would not, but we all would hear a message that we could all do so ("from management trainee to vice president," in the words of the job application at Enterprise.com) and that would inspire us to sacrifice for our own good. If the company hired 7,000 college graduates each year but there were only 7,500 Level II employees, there had to be a winnowing process.

At three in the morning, with no letup in Dennis's inharmonious snoring, I quietly packed my bag, walked down the hall to the lobby, and got my own room. The next day Dennis apologized, and Zoë said she'd cover my room.

NATE, WHO SAT on my left, started off the week of training with a silver-and-blue can of Red Bull set on his desk like a totem. Nate had just graduated from the University of Arizona, where he was both pledge of the year and house manager of his fraternity, Sigma Chi. Within seconds of shaking hands with me, he referred to his college football team: "Yeah, dude. Wildcats!" When I made note of his apparent fondness for Red Bull, Nate told me that he actually preferred to drink yerba maté, which he bought on the Internet and had shipped directly from Argentina. It works as an efficient hangover reliever, but more important, he said, "it gives you a boost that's not as harsh and short-lived as coffee." During our week at

the hotel, he drank until late at night and then rose at six in the
morning to hit the mediocre hotel gym, and he was typically one of
the first to arrive in class.

A fellow classmate nicknamed Nate "The Machine" for his ability to recall information. He had an encyclopedic memory for the
material we learned each day and retained every last Enterprise
fact. Nate dismissed the idea that he had any aptitude for memorization and told us that it was just that the test-taking abilities he
gained in college were still fresh. At lunch one day, Nate, who was
just 22, explained to me the intricate differences between the HMO,
EPO, and PPO health insurance policies that Enterprise offered us
as employees. He'd showed up at his first Enterprise interview
having memorized the company's eight founding values. Soon we
would all memorize them: *Great things happen when we listen . . . to
our customers and each other. . . . We work hard . . . and we reward hard
work. . . . Customer service is our way of life. . . . Enterprise is a fun and
friendly place where teamwork rules.*

Nate was organized and was planning his future. He drove a
two-door Honda Civic EX with tinted windows that he kept waxed
and shining. He told me that he would drive that car "into the
ground," then drive one of the company cars offered to any Level II
managerial employee, all the while saving up for his ultimate ride.
In the short term, he would pay back his father for a $3,000 loan the
previous summer that allowed him to explore Europe for two
months. On the trip he had traveled through 16 cities and met rela-
tives in his native Greece. He also ran with the bulls in Pamplona,
something that others in class did not really understand until he
explained his "appetite for extreme sports." He also planned to buy
a beveled TAG Heuer watch, studded with diamonds and mother-
of-pearl, like the one worn by Tiger Woods and sold at Macy's for
$1,600. Though this seemed a questionable purchase, seeing that
we were paid about $800 per week, it was obvious that for Nate, the

watch would provide a steppingstone to future status purchases and would stand as a monument to the station in life he had attained. Nate was an impressive catch for Enterprise—a joiner, a believer, a person who had bought the American notion of fulfillment through organization and consumption. I overheard that he had been slotted for a future management position. Zoë told him: "With the type of outgoing personality you have, your branch is a great match." Nate was going to be based in Oakland, in an area not far from where he grew up. He had recently watched a DVD that was circulating called *Oakland Gone Wild* that showed illegal car rallies on city streets. He told me about the delirious crowds that come out to watch these "sideshows" in Oakland and that people become "deindividualized" and turn to "groupthink."

On the way to class each day, I stopped at a roadside coffee hut run by three Japanese-American women who were a picture of efficiency as they served up coffee and bagels for worker bees like me. One morning a scruffy woman ambling down the street looked at me walking out with my hot coffee in hand and said, "You look like you are a successful businessman." I smiled and tried to see myself from the outside, dressed in a blue suit, and pondered how fully in character I was, in front of this stranger and my coworkers. Each morning I was mindful not to be late. Students who were late ended up sitting outside the classroom all morning, locked out and ignored by Zoë so that they might learn a lesson. "Look, team," she said, "this is not college anymore. No more sleeping through that chem class because you don't feel like going. If you don't open the branch, gang, nobody else is going to."

During the week, Zoë asked a few of us what cars we drove. Akiko, we learned, had a 1990 Toyota Celica, and the vintage of her vehicle became the butt of more than one of Zoë's jokes. She seemed more impressed by Gordon, who told us that he had a new 2005 Chevy Silverado. "An '05? Right on, Gordon," said Zoë. Zoë seemed like a sweet woman at heart, but no doubt years of drinking in the hardened and bland Enterprise culture had changed her, made her more like it.

Zoë liked to say, "Hey, gang" to call our attention to a particular fact she was teaching us or to underline a point she was making. She was a strong teacher. Many of her most valuable lessons were taught informally, as asides that seemed to tumble out accidentally during her otherwise tightly run lessons. She offhandedly mentioned things such as a regional vice president who had recently retired at age 36. She told us, by way of personal experience, about the yearly trip to Orlando that all 7,500 managerial employees are invited to each May, a four-day party with free Budweiser, the consumption of which was said to rival that during the Super Bowl. These were asides, yes, but they were meant to entice us, to dangle carrots in front of us. Zoë also beautifully referenced the founding values, such as "Great things happen when we listen to our customers," to summarize lessons. And soon enough, we fell in step. "What's the single biggest advantage we have over our competition?" Zoë asked us. "Our people," we told her.

Zoë had been with the company for eight years. She joined after a stint in the Canadian federal police force after college. She applied and was accepted, she told us, at both business and law schools but never went, and because of the awesome upward trajectory of her Enterprise career, she never regretted it. She said she had learned and earned more at Enterprise than she would have elsewhere. Like the stories she told us, she was herself an example of how we could succeed at Enterprise. We could all end up like her, with days spent seemingly as our own bosses shaping a crew of trainees. Like a drill sergeant, she took us to task, often calling out dress code violations. She told Gordon to pull up his suit pants when he sagged them gangster-like, and complimented Amir that he "dressed like an area manager—sharp." People who wore wrinkled clothes would be passed over for promotions, she told us. She rode Dennis all week about his hipster facial hair, and he continually ducked her requests with silly excuses: "Um, like, I tried to shave it last night, but my razor was too dull . . ." On the last day he finally submitted to her wishes and shaved his goatlike soul patch.

We ended our week of classroom training with a championship game. Split into three teams of four, we trudged downstairs into a large boardroom. Dennis joked that we were joining Donald Trump's TV series *The Apprentice,* but the décor betrayed this; the room was decorated with motivational posters and cheap furniture probably delivered from the OfficeMax store across the freeway. The pizza Zoë ordered arrived, and we took our seats around the large oval faux-mahogany table. Questions followed:

- What does LOFR stand for? *Lube, oil, filter, rotate.*
- What is negligent entrustment? *Renting to an unlicensed or unsafe driver.*
- What does ESQi stand for? *Enterprise Service Quality Index.*
- Define "running tight." *When the branch is running at very high occupancy and very few vehicles are available to rent.*

This game was preparing us for the final exam we would have to take in 10 days. My ex-roommate Dennis asked, "What happens if we fail?" and we all laughed. "Way to raise the bar there, Dennis," said Zoë. She told us that if we were late for the exam, we would be asked to leave Enterprise. If we failed the test, however, we would not be terminated, just required to report directly to the regional vice president. "It's not the ideal way to meet your RVP for the first time," Zoë said. Every time she was up, Yolanda, the apprentice creative visualizer, answered each question right without turning to her teammates. The inter-team trash talking was lively, and Zoë said sarcastically: "No, we don't hire people who are competitive here at Enterprise!"

There were certainly painfully long hours, but in general the week of training was surprisingly unboring, in large part thanks to Zoë's strengths as a teacher and her ability to engage us. On paper, her job was to train us, but she was also a cheerleader for Enterprise, the brand, and her strongest value to the company was no doubt her ability to proselytize, to bring us into the huddle. Despite my better judgment, I was starting to believe in Enterprise myself. With Zoë's work done, we were off to our branches.

BRANCHING OUT

My branch was a no-frills square building, the seventeenth branch opened in the Bay Area. The inside was paved in worn-out carpet tiles, some of which peeled from the floor below. We had a small, unadorned sitting room for customers. It was a timeless, placeless industrial space. Inside there were five of us: Bert, the manager, was in his late twenties and had a jowly face and brown hair; L.J., the assistant manager, was a squat woman with the look of a grown-up baby; Clara, management assistant, was tall with movie-star long brown hair; and Abe was a slim Chinese man who nervously laughed a lot and was six months ahead of me as a management trainee. He had an extended left pinkie fingernail in flagrant violation of our dress code that stated that nails "must be cleaned and well trimmed."

We parked cars in a back lot encircled by a cyclone fence. Richard and Carlos, our on-site "car preps," vacuumed and washed the cars between uses. Their area was surprisingly ill maintained, with wood siding that had been water damaged and a couple of vacuums duct-taped together. They had erected a small shrine of effluvia left behind in cars: stray hairbrushes, bumper stickers, mini-mart thermos mugs, tree-shaped cardboard air fresheners, and assorted plastic McDonald's Happy Meal action figures.

During the first week at my branch, our workload was subdued. The week before, a flash flood in the county had totaled hundreds of cars—both Enterprise and private cars. Owners with insurance quickly snapped up all the rentals we had. We pulled in cars from as many branches as we could, but even a week later we still didn't have much to rent to customers. We were *running tight*.

On my first day, I had lunch with our area manager, a Vietnamese-American woman named Yvette. Yvette was several rungs up the ladder: She managed three branches, and my manager reported directly to her. She was in her early thirties, dressed fashionably, and gave off an air of supreme organization. She told me that my future at Enterprise was up to me and that if there was anything I needed, she would be there for me. "My door is always open," she said, loosely quoting one of Enterprise's eight founding values. Back in the branch proper, Clara would serve as my "branch buddy." She had worked at our branch for just over a year and would show me the ropes and help me fill out the lengthy training assignment due back to Zoë the next week.

Among other responsibilities, teaching me how to navigate Enterprise's ancient computer system, which I failed to master at training camp, was Clara's job. The client-server technology was a relic of the 1970s. On this office computer system, there was no such thing as Windows. Enterprise seemed a frugal company through and through. The system was called RALPH for "rapid and logical paper handler." In 1978 it might have been an advance on filing systems of the day, but by 2006 RALPH was neither rapid nor logical. The biggest stumbling block on the job was figuring out just how to operate a computer system launched before the bulk of the company's employees were born. RALPH had green type on a black background, and you had to punch in commands and check lines; there was little use for a mouse. I spent most of my first week trying to remember all the commands and strange needs of this outdated and archaic system. When I checked my email at home each night, I felt as if I had returned from work at a Cold War bomb silo.

Instead of engaging in multimillion-dollar information technology upgrades, Enterprise had made the decision to train employees to use these old computers. Other rewards of this system for the company: external email was not widespread at the company and we had no distracting Internet access. Though the system would not last forever, our links to the outside world were constrained. We were trapped in our own controlled environment, just as the occupants of Biosphere II were in theirs. And just maybe this entrenched frugality was why Enterprise was soaring while its competitors were slogging along. In fact, Enterprise had become the largest player in the rental car industry by successfully exploiting the insurance-replacement market against number-two Hertz, which had focused on airport rentals. (Enterprise had more than 600,000 cars in its fleet and almost 6,000 locations in the United States, 90 percent of which were not at airports.)

The company rewards those who master its prehistoric computer system and learn to enter contracts quickly. My coworker L.J. said that her own record for signing customers to contracts was 315 in a month and that the high-water mark in our region was 345 for an insanely fast woman at a nearby branch.

During the first week, I had homework. One of the many exercises on the list was called phone shopping. To phone-shop, you went into the back room of the office and placed phone calls to Enterprise's competitors—the local offices of Hertz, Avis, and Budget.

When our doppelgangers answered the phone, we had license to create a persona: "Hi. You got any of those little, um, small, um, minivans? Oh, you do? Okay, I need one now. How much is that going to run me?"

We did this, I was told, to ascertain the availability of competitors' vehicles. If we knew that the neighboring three rental agencies were completely out of SUVs, and we had three, we would raise the rates on our SUVs. Customers who reserved one of our rental cars on the Internet would almost always get a better rate than calling or walking into a branch. Still, our phone rang all day. By the second day I was not at all self-conscious about reaching for the phone before my colleagues: "Thank you for calling Enterprise Rent-A-Car. My name is Alex. How may I help you?" It was certain that among the many calls we received, many were phone-shoppers both real and fake, and many were no doubt Enterprise's own quality-control people.

L.J. was my favorite colleague. She was in her mid-twenties and wore polyester pantsuits and side-zip black boots to work. She seemed to have stalled out in the assistant manager position, but having been with the company for five years, she was filled with on-the-job wisdom. She was a perfect Enterprise specimen and a big believer in the Enterprise experience. Whenever I got in a pinch, she was happy to keep an eye on my computer screen or even take over. L.J. told me that when I was signing a customer to a contract, I should move from behind the desk to the parking lot before attempting to sell them insurance. She called this "moving to a neutral territory," where I could stand "shoulder to shoulder" with my customer. She told me that I should go over insurance first and foremost with customers; otherwise, I was bound to lose their interest.

"You have to feel out the customer and get a sense of who they are and what kind of a person they are," she said. And she told me to try different ways to sell insurance. She said that she had "changed her spiel five million times in five years. You don't want the customer to think you are a machine. You have to sound human." She told me that once in a while you have to craft stories. Say a car was not on the lot but a customer was: You might tell the customer that the car is just getting a quick oil change ("We just want to make sure that the car is running as well as it can for you") and that it would be back in an hour. Then you want to try to up-sell them to another car that we *do* have. "It's tricky, but you'll get the hang of it," she said. *Two truths and one lie*, I thought to myself.

And so once I had signed a customer into a contract, I would go to the parking lot in front where I would conduct a "trunk to trunk" review of the car and note any dings or scratches. There, in the parking lot, I would try to sell our customers up to three types of coverage. We were told not to use the word *insurance*. Our training texts defined the damage waiver as "not insurance" but "an agreement between you (the customer) and Enterprise in which Enterprise waives the right to impose a financial obligation on you if you return the vehicle with damages." Like this nondefinition filled with disingenuous language, insurance selling was filled with ambiguity. Our goal was to have a customer sign up for all three pieces of coverage we offered—this was called "trips," for triple coverage. Selling insurance at Enterprise was, strangely enough, one of the few places for on-the-job creativity: a time to explore alternate approaches, to throw various attempts out there and see what stuck. Because of the lack of standards, I got the feeling that management really did not care how we sold it, just that we did it. Somewhere along the line, it was clear, an employee transformed from the textbook trainee into a creative employee who figured out the shortcuts and just what was necessary to get the job done.

Unlike L.J., my branch buddy Clara appeared to use just one way to sell: affecting a passive-aggressive tone. "And how will you be covering this car?" she would ask, always speaking in a higher-pitched voice with a lot of "okays?" thrown in. When she inevitably heard that the customer would use his or her own insurance, she would say, "Can you tell me how much your deductible is?" and make a note of it on the contract. The deductible was of no consequence—it was more a way to get the customer concerned, to compare paying $16 per day with $500.

After working at Enterprise, I rented a number of cars from the company—in Boston, New York, Vancouver, and Spokane—and noticed variations on the bullying technique. In the classic method, an employee would ask, "So will you be getting the basic or the full coverage today?" making it sound as if you needed at least one form, when in fact you didn't. Often they'd start with a "positive assumption" such as "You're going with our full coverage, right?" Customers were saved by the "Three 'No' Policy" that Enterprise subscribed to: If you hear a customer say no three times, you need to back off.

L.J. was our biggest seller of insurance and could sell most of her customers on some sort of coverage. Employees in a regional area competed weekly on "protection stats" for $50 and $100 in cash. We would get emails like this one: "Team, these are some scary stats! I know you guys can do much better. Shake it off and show me what you guys are all about. Good luck! Yvette."

My approach was to assume that a customer did not want insurance and to leave the door open for the rare customer who did. But when I sold my first "full trips," I felt a surge of adrenaline. I was finally pushing my way out from the cold and into the Enterprise culture. It happened so effortlessly, so easily that I wondered how much was skill and how much was luck. After that sale, I casually showed L.J. my completed contract and her face lit up. When our manager came around, L.J. told him, "Alex got trips," and I beamed. I was now, for the first time, a positive data point on a graph, a part of the all-important sales information feeding into the corporate matrix.

Another day, one of my customers requested an upgrade from one car to another, and that extra six dollars a day qualified me to enter an area-wide contest that would identify the employee responsible for the most upgrades. Again L.J. entered my name on a form as I scrawled "Everything is a contest in this place" on a Post-it and shoved it into my trousers pocket. Taking notes like this was a constant challenge at each job. I found different media that fit in at each workplace—package notices at UPS, Post-its at Enterprise— and always had to make sure nobody happened on any of my scribblings.

When I was working at the branch, I would leave my house at 6:50 in the morning and get home at about seven each evening. I was impressed by my coworkers' sacrifice, their willingness to work the 60-hour-a-week schedules (including most Saturdays) that went into overtime daily and ate up most of their waking lives. Though I had no plans to remain at Enterprise for long, I knew my colleagues planned to stick it out. Though there are no public records, we were told that Enterprise has a 96 percent employee retention rate for the first 90 days, and that this rate remains strong for the first year.

Occasionally I imagined what would happen if I stayed and played the Enterprise game. I could try to work my way out of my lowly position and on to the next level. Maybe upward mobility would come quickly to me, and I would excel, and the financial gains through profit sharing and greater responsibilities that came with managing others and managing a fleet of cars would be intoxicating and supply me with what I would need to keep at it. But in truth I was not a natural member of this tribe. I have a hard time sacrificing myself for a cause I don't believe in and wasn't interested in mastering the art of selling insurance. When I put myself in the place of my coworkers, I was claustrophobic, scared off by all the bullshit I would have to endure to move ahead. I had the luxury of knowing that I could leave at any time—for me the job was not real. The only way I might have stayed would have been as an endurance challenge, to see how quickly I could have ascended the ranks. Despite the fact that I could have bailed out easily, sometimes it was hard to remember I was just visiting, that I was a tourist and that Zoë and all of my colleagues lived in that world.

Time moved slowly at the branch, and I had a lot of time to look at my watch and wait. I looked forward to getting dispatched to pick up or drop off a customer. A decade before, an employee in Florida thought of a way to differentiate Enterprise from its competition, by picking up and dropping off customers. It seemed to be working. As part of this process, we learned in training that it's best to pick up a customer in a nicer, larger car than the one they rented, and use the discrepancy as a means to up-sell the customer. I always selected the nicest car on our lot when I drove out—one day it was a shiny Mercedes CL280 with 55 miles on it, another day a Chrysler 300 with a wide grille. After I had dropped off a customer, I would give myself a five-minute break to enjoy some solitude. When I was out of the office, time became my own again, and it felt good. One day I went to a Jeep dealership to retrieve a woman and her child. When I pulled up in the Chrysler 300, she said: "Wow, I didn't expect to be picked up by a well-dressed man driving a fancy car." My suit had just won over another customer.

Until I had the system dialed in, it was unlikely that I would win over many such customers by my behavior. One customer named Jonathan reminded me of myself by the way he dressed and talked. He worked for Kaplan, the test preparatory program, which paid for his car and full coverage. I sent him off in a Mitsubishi Galant, and he called a few days later with a question that I was able to answer. When he returned at the end of the week, someone else checked him in and asked whether he was "completely satisfied," to which he said: "Alex set me up." I was appreciative of the call-out in front of my team.

One day I picked up an overweight man named John. On the ride back, we had an interesting conversation about topics as varied as the reception quality of his cell phone and whether the second album by the North Mississippi Allstars lived up to the first. As I was checking him in, he presented a discount coupon and also mentioned that he had signed up for our weekend special. My coworker L.J. looked over and said that he could not use two discounts, just one. She was adamant that he could not double down on the discounts; he was adamant that he could. L.J. took over and I stood on the sidelines wondering who would triumph. Without ever getting angry, John spent 15 minutes on the phone with corporate customer service until he was vindicated. L.J., who had been fighting over $20, said she was sorry. I walked him out to his Toyota Camry and also apologized. We might have bonded when we were driving along in *neutral territory*, but it had shattered in the office. He got in and drove away.

Another customer called in to request an SUV, and after I told him that we didn't have any, he got angry. His car dealership, he said, promised him an SUV while his car was being fixed. Later in the day, I went to this dealership to pick him up. The dealership, called Park Royale, sprawled over an area some two city blocks wide. The dealership serviced and sold GM cars, including Chevrolets and Hummers. When they needed a GM car for a customer, our branch supplied it. We even had a small branch inside the dealership that we occasionally staffed, and I was told that I might run this microbranch at some point. With more than 70 multihued Hummers on the lot, there were enough to supply an attack force invading a small nation. The guy I picked up was white and in his late thirties, pudgy, and affecting a rap-star look (baggy pants, collectible Nike high-tops, hooded sweatshirt). As we drove back to the branch, he talked incessantly on his cell phone to a succession of friends. I overheard that he had filed suit against Hummer over mechanical problems. He called his gambling buddy to get advice on what color Hummer his lawyer should request. "What color party bus do you want, dude?" he asked. His friend suggested black, and he worried out loud that it would require weekly cleaning. "I'll do it if black will grab a lot of attention," he said without irony. When we got to the branch to fill out a contract, he again bemoaned our lack of Hummers. "Look, I know I am a pain-in-the-ass customer," he said.

In each workplace, there were places that customers are not meant to venture, places such as the back of the truck at UPS. When an older guy walked into our Enterprise branch one day and turned to my coworker L.J. and asked, "What do we have out back?" as he strolled through our office and into the back car lot, I assumed he was a member of the Enterprise management team or one of the "hikers," a crew of retired men who delivered new cars to us. This guy walked out back, took a look around at our collection of cars—Chevy Aveos, Dodge Neons, a VW Jetta—walked back inside, and made small talk with L.J., who introduced me.

"Are you new to Enterprise? Did you come here from another branch?" asked the guy. He was wearing an untucked pink polo shirt, a pair of mildly faded blue jeans, white sneakers, and a yarmulke.

"Yes," I told him, "I just started this week."

"I've been told that I have helped many careers here by providing recommendations. I may be able to help you in time as well," he said.

The man told me that he was an accountant registered in 35 states. We chatted for a few minutes before he abruptly took the conversation in an unexpected direction: "I was trained in all aspects by Israeli intelligence," he said, leaving me locked in his gaze and somewhat confused.

"Does he work for Enterprise?" I asked L.J. when he had left. Harold Andrews, it turned out, was the longest-running customer of our branch. He was not one of us; he was one of them. Andrews was far from a typical customer but a customer nonetheless. His tenure had outlasted that of all the employees, even the car prep named Richard, who had been there more than a decade. Andrews had been renting from Enterprise, at that branch, for more than 13 years, and loyally returned each Thursday at precisely 1 PM to renew the agreement on his vehicle, which he rented at a rock-bottom, grandfathered rate of $99 a week. According to L.J., the benefit to him had something to do with structure and grounding for his obsessive-compulsive disorder. He drove the same car week after week, until Enterprise sold the car and he was forced to rent another, newer vehicle. I expressed amazement at the fact that he rented all year, and Bert pulled out a calculator to determine that Andrews spent more than $5,000 a year with us.

When Andrews returned the following week, I saw him walk in and I approached the counter as he did. He smiled at me. "Hello, Alex. How is Enterprise? Are they training you well?" He had the vocal intonations and pauses of Alec Guinness as Obi-Wan Kenobi. "Thank you, Alex, but L.J. will help me. When you have learned more, you too will be able to help me. For now, L.J. will help me. Thank you, Alex." And so L.J. did help him, and she dispatched me outside to wash Andrews's gunmetal gray Dodge Neon and to vacuum a car lightly strewn with his belongings. "Hold your nose," L.J. cautioned. I found no evidence in the car to complete the pic-ture of an obsessive-compulsive accountant–secret agent, just a few FedEx packets filled with legal papers.

Andrews was the über-customer. Zoë had talked a lot about our creating "customers for life," and I had found one. He was a gross exaggeration of this very idea, but he was the unique and complete fulfillment of an Enterprise corporate mission. Our job was to make walk-in customers into Andrewses.

On a Friday morning Clara and I took a doughnut run to visit about 15 of the auto body shops and car dealerships that sent us much of our business. We drove around and delivered doughnuts that we had piled into Enterprise-branded doughnut boxes. Clara said she had put her name in for an opening as an assistant manager at another branch. She told me as we drove that I would soon take on the relationships she had made with all of the people we were meeting. I shook hands and met the various desk-bound "service advisors" as Clara gleaned nuggets of wisdom to add to her repertoire of small talk: *Curt is in Vegas with his girlfriend, so be sure to ask about that next time; Lofrano and Son Auto Body has a backlog of three months on account of the storm.*

HELLA RED BULL

The next Monday I was crossing the San Francisco Bay as the sun rose, heading back to headquarters. After our first weeks on the job, our original class of 12 students and a couple of other management trainees returned to regional headquarters to sit for our final exam. If we did not make it by 8 AM sharp, Zoë told us, we would be cut from training and sent home. The final exam had 25 questions that were quite easy. The questions tested rote memorization, except for the last four short essay-style questions.

I was done in 20 minutes and joined my classmates in the break room to trade stories of our first weeks on the job. We had fanned out across the nine Bay Area counties: Dennis to Vallejo, Nate to Oakland, Ted to San Francisco. I found a support group. Keith, who worked in Monterey, described average nights finishing at 8 PM.

After work he would head home to a crash pad he shared with three other recently graduated college friends. His room was the living room, which made it hard to sleep. "I've been drinking hella Red Bull," he said, and left it at that. Another guy shared his own method of selling insurance to unsuspecting customers and regaled us with stories of selling "trips": "Dude, I'd, like, rattle off a bunch of stuff and, like, totally confuse them, and then I'd, like, say, 'So, you want full coverage?' And they're like, 'Okay,' " said Allan.

"Don't confuse them," Chinh said earnestly.

After break we went back to our training room, and Zoë read through our tests briefly, pausing to note that a surprisingly high number of us had gotten the first question wrong—the year in which Jack Taylor founded Enterprise. The correct answer was 1957, not 1948, as I had written down.

"Nate got it wrong, Jeff got it wrong, Alex got it wrong. Come on, guys!"

Zoë opened up the room for discussion. "Stories, stories, anyone? The good, the bad, the ugly?" We were like a small, lightly armored expeditionary force back from reconnaissance. People now had real-life experiences to draw from; things were no longer vague or hypo-thetical. We went around the room and shared. Our tales were surprisingly different. Ted said he spent most days locked in place behind the counter waiting on customers at a busy San Francisco branch. Edward drove around all day picking up customers. A Ni-gerian guy, Ajani, who sat on my right, was studying engineering by night at San Francisco State and had been placed at the airport, one of the more stressful places to work, with its constant influx of cus-tomers and long hours. He wore a suit jacket several sizes too large.

"How's it going at the airport?" Zoë wanted to know. Ajani de-scribed long days with cold winds blowing in from the Bay. "Every day, I think, *I want to quit*," he said in a candid tone that caught people by surprise. Zoë took his remarks in stride and offered positive feedback. A fellow classmate also leaned over and shared his own thoughts: "Dude, it will get better."

Zoë said the fatigue we were all feeling would dissipate over time. "It will take six months for you guys to adjust to the job," she told us. She said we would all figure out how to make our days easier by finding gyms and dry cleaners right near home so we could effectively use our homes as pivot points as the job moved us around and we were transferred to other branches.

We spent an hour at the end of training talking about sexual harassment in the workplace. Zoë told us that because of the young age of employees and the many single people, harassment issues did arise. During this section, Zoë betrayed the general message she had been feeding us that there was room for all of us to grow at Enterprise. She said that the bad apples should be flushed out, that it didn't matter how high on the corporate ladder the offending sexual harasser was because "there are five million other people coming up through the ranks who can replace" this guy.

True to protocol, we learned about sexual harassment by role-playing and by exploring solutions to what Zoë told us were real-life cases of harassment in the workplace. "Each one of these cases, gang, was something I saw out there as a manager, okay?" One such hypothetical involved a party at the home of an Enterprise employee. Ajani had been with the company longer than the rest of us, and he told me he had been to many such parties at one of his co-workers' houses. "There are tons of females," he said. He recounted tales of married women from the branch grabbing him as they disco-danced around. "It's okay with me," he said, smiling. "They are not harassing me."

After a few more lessons and some paperwork, we went back to our branches and to what was becoming more of a regular grind. During what was my last week, I was invited to two dinners, one of them related to the Enterprise Service Quality Index, or ESQi, a number that gauges the quality of customer service at each branch. Each month an independent survey group hired by Enterprise's corporate offices calls 33 customers of each branch. When they reach a customer, they ask about the customer's level of satisfaction with the branch's service. A branch receives one point for each customer who reports that he or she was "completely satisfied." A branch that receives 33 points for three months in a row then has a three-month trailing average of 99, or a perfect score. Most branches receive monthly scores of about 27, and the corporate ESQi average hovers at about 80. The number has profound consequences. If a branch score is under the corporate average, no individual employee is eligible for a transfer or promotion. And thanks to the system of averaging three months' worth of scores, it can take six months to climb out of a subaverage trough.

The branch that my ex-roommate had shipped off to, in Vallejo, had an ESQi of 68. There, I imagined, he would encounter a corporate branch of no return, a branch resembling Kurtz's heads-on-stakes *Heart of Darkness* hideout. On the other end of the spectrum, the branches with the highest scores each month are invited by the region's top executives to an ESQi dinner. My branch had been the winner the previous month (before I arrived), with an impressive score of 94, so we joined a smaller branch (of just two employees) that had won in the 50-cars-or-fewer class. On the face of it, it seemed a trifle unfair that I would land at a place so highly rated, while my roommate was at a disadvantage from the outset. But we had all been chosen by our immediate supervisors.

For the ESQi dinner we met at a contemporary roadhouse along the highway and were joined by John Davidson, the regional rental vice president. Davidson was a family man in his early fifties with thinning hair and a weary, athletic face. This dinner was the first time I had seen the members of my branch assembled off-site, and I felt as if we were some kind of contemporary corporate family. My coworker Abe sat next to L.J., who treated him like a little brother. *Are you sure you are not drinking too much? Do you really think you can eat that whole plate? Smile. Tuck in that shirt. Shake hands with our boss's boss. Look him in the eye. Thank him for dinner.* In the role of patriarch, the regional vice president ordered several bottles of wine for the table, encouraged us to order whatever we wanted, and regaled us with tales from the trenches. Stories stuck close to themes of overintoxication and overeating. "I remember one ESQi dinner," he said, "when a guy ordered a seventy-five-ounce porterhouse steak. I am not shitting you." Someone asked him how often customer complaints got to him, and he said that five calls got to his desk each day and he talked to one to three customers a week. "Eighty percent of the time, I give the customer what they want," he said.

Bert, my manager, sat next to Davidson, and the two engaged in a serious discussion. L.J. told me she thought that in five years our manager would be managing on a regional basis. She said that he knew what he was doing and advised me that I could learn a lot from him, that he understood the car business very well. Davidson and Bert recalled attending the yearly Enterprise meeting in Orlando, when the corporation's owners entertain the troops by, among other things, renting out Disney World. Someone mentioned the performance of Smash Mouth, the band invited the year before. Living up to the band's name, its leader had talked ill of the company at the live performance (saying he'd rather rent from Budget and yelling out profanities) before he was forced to leave the stage.

We clapped when my manager announced that Clara, who had just turned 25, had been promoted to assistant manager and would soon move to another branch. "Welcome to Level II!" he said. Clara, now up two rungs, could barely contain her excitement. I had been told that our branch was a stepping-off point for area managers. I felt like the black sheep of the family and inwardly recoiled at the thought that my branch might have pinned its future plans on my ascendance—and I would be leaving shortly. I was invited to another celebratory dinner that week, for the region's top performers, gauged by their ability to sell "coverage." L.J., of our branch, was going, and all new employees like me had been invited as well to show what we should work hard to attain and, likely, to provide an audience for the celebration.

In the course of this job-hopping journey, telling my managers I was quitting was never easy. I was an enthusiastic learner eager to do the job, so it made little sense that I would turn tail one day and bail out. In each case I felt that I was letting the group down; I had invaded their space and they had devoted precious on-the-job time to train me as part of the team. But I soon left Enterprise. I'd been boxed in by the long hours, and I then was free again.

A few weeks after I quit, I found a curious website called FailingEnterprise.com. It was amateurishly designed and mostly a wide-ranging discussion board, but the subject matter was serious. In the closed world of Enterprise, there was no room for nonbelievers, but one disgruntled ex-customer named Barry Stiefel had penetrated the Enterprise veil by putting up this simple website a few years before in the hope of shaming Enterprise into changing its ways. "Within a week or two, the site got indexed by Google," he told me, "and then I started getting all this email from former employees, saying, in effect, 'You think it's bad being a customer at Enterprise, you should try working there!' There were so many emails pouring in that I decided to create a discussion board, just to see what might happen. It took off."

By the time I was at Enterprise, Stiefel had mailed postcards to Enterprise branches and invited employees to participate in the discussion board. Many workers surfaced, some guarded, some excited to share in discussions that rarely took place at work. In the closed world of Enterprise, there was no room for dissent, but online, people picked apart the pieces. According to Stiefel, while many defended Enterprise, other employees who read the postings came to realize that the long hours, low pay, stress, poor working conditions, and brainwashing they experienced were company-wide and not exclusive to them or their branch. Many discussion threads were about that very fact. Job applicants were also paying heed to the site and bailing out of the application process, while current employees were quitting earlier than they would have because of what they read on the discussion board.

I'd come to think that a large part of why so many people work at Enterprise was because they believed in what the company stood for—whether it was the eight founding values we were all taught, forced to memorize, and encouraged to keep in our wallets like true evangelists—or, more likely, a belief in the possibilities of personal achievement and financial success. But here, current and former employees were coming to terms with their own levels of belief. Discussions included both the still faithful and those who had renounced their faith. Some people were making sense of their experience, some were rejoicing in leaving, and some defended their jobs and the company, while still others inquired about the benefits of applying.

Postings came from all over the world, with names such as *Slavenomore* and *ExErac656*. Postings ranged from the humorous to the serious, from short to lengthy. "I left the cult recently," noted one poster tersely. Another congratulated someone for quitting: "Welcome back from the dark side!" Those few who defended Enterprise were roundly called names such as "upper management green bleeders."

Former employees commiserated about the dress code. "Who here can remember losing a perfectly good tie to the airport Super Vac?" In one of the more popular threads, titled "My ERAC Story," former employees shared the details of their work experiences. The exchanges were a back-and-forth between a smaller number of people defending the experience (and the training and skills they gained) and many others denouncing it for the lack of life-work balance, Enterprise's system of lying, and for being a sacrifice not worth it.

Goingforward wrote that he was fired but realized the experience had a value:

> I guess what I'm trying to say is that Enterprise gave me some marketable skills. While I have a lot of animosity for the way I was treated, I am most definitely better off now than I would have been if I stayed there. I probably know 20 people who have left E either on their own or through a termination and I can't think of one who isn't doing better today than they were then. So never let anyone tell you that you suck, and reach for the stars. You can do it!

One characteristic post noted:

> There is a reason why everyone in the company is young. There is nowhere to go within the company. Once you hit manager, your options become very slim. Next up is the area manager spot. When a position like this becomes available, 10 people interview for it. You can be stuck as branch manager forever. People eventually realize that they are maxed out in their careers and they move on and the company then hires more college kids to take your place.

The voices on the board defending Enterprise chiefly used the argument that those leaving negative comments were not career-driven enough to stick it out and that the hard work weeds out the weak and promotes the strong. Another former worker wrote:

My ERAC story spans 7 years. I started in a group a loooooong way away from the group I just left. I performed well and worked my butt off and became a superstar. Let's just say shortly after beginning there I bled green and was sold on the dream of six figures in six years. It began to take a toll on my health, my sanity, and my relationship with my wife. I spoke with my upper management and they kept telling me to think about the career opportunities that would be waiting for me if I just kept working harder and harder.

In another thread, people posted about the day they quit. One guy compared the day after he quit to Christmas. Another wrote:

Leaving ERAC was an absolutely great feeling. . . . Just being able to go for a drink with my friends after work, not be feeling tired all the time, no more pointless meetings, no more 60-hour weeks ever again. I can honestly say that the decision I made to leave ERAC was the best one of my whole life.

FailingEnterprise.com had strains of a post-cult debriefing center for the many who had drunk the ERAC Kool-Aid. Much of what I read in the postings echoed thoughts I'd had while I was still locked into the job, that this was a company whose corporate culture constantly emphasized upward mobility even though such mobility was not necessarily a realistic promise for all employees. If I were to post my own ERAC story, it would be a short one, though it would resemble the others: I was hired and trained. I rented cars. But I never believed; I never bled the all-powerful green.

FOUR

INTO THE FOLD

Our purpose: Every day, Gap Inc. honors the original reason for founding this company: We're passionate that you be you. We make it easy for you to express your personal style throughout your life. When we're at our best, this purpose comes through in everything we do. In how we help our customers find their personal style. In how our stores look and feel and work. In how we treat each other. In how we work together.

—Gap training documents

The Gap men's department where I was assigned sprawled across a room 200 feet long and 40 feet wide. An escalator from the first floor delivered customers adjacent to a central stainless-steel counter and cash registers. The room was lit by fluorescent lights strung from the ceiling and had artificial blond-wood flooring.

I arrived on my first day wearing a pair of pleated khakis that were a little baggy and a pressed collared shirt; they were the only clothes I had that did not violate Gap's dress code. Compared with my new coworkers who actually owned a lot of Gap clothes and knew which garments were cool, I looked like a dork, like a Gap customer dressed to work in a cubicle, not a salesman ready to sell clothes.

Alberto, my coach, was a big guy who wore an untucked blue-and-white-striped button-down shirt and faded denim jeans cut at the ankles and splayed just so over a pair of imposing size 16 Nikes. As Alberto led me to our department, we passed a sign that said, among other things, "You are the brand: Present yourself with integrity and professionalism," and "Smile. Body language is worth a thousand words."

Once we arrived at the men's department, Alberto threw me into what felt like a wide-open pool where I had to learn how to swim. He told me to wander the floor, help customers, approach them, and answer their questions. He told me that I should avoid asking customers questions that could be answered with *yes* or *no*, and instead to leave them open-ended. I was fairly certain that any customer knew more than I did about our clothing inventory. I told Alberto that I didn't know much, and he smiled and said, "It's the only way to learn, dude," as he turned away and sent me out to stroll.

Interviewing and hiring at Gap was quite easy: I filled out a paper application at the store, was invited to a group interview, and then had a 10-minute follow-up with an in-store hiring manager. But never during Gap's interview was my passion for Gap products evaluated. I wasn't convinced that this was something necessary for employment, because Gap needed to hire scores of workers with the approach of the holiday season. For me a Gap job was alluring because it was a generic position selling a generic product. Given that Gap had seemingly lost its one-time buzz, I wanted to see what it was that attracted the other workers to the company and what made them stay. I had a sense that it would be boring, but I didn't know the half of it.

GAP, A NATIVE San Francisco enterprise, was founded in 1969 by real estate developer Don Fisher and his wife Doris. According to corporate lore, the two could not find a decent place to buy their kids jeans and music in one place. Early on, Gap (always *Gap*, never *the Gap*) sold chiefly records and tapes and clothing brands such as Levi's. The store promoted itself with the catchy slogan "Fall into the Gap." By 2006 Gap had grown from the Fishers' modest Ocean Avenue store to an empire grossing $19 billion a year, with more than 3,000 stores in all 50 states and five other countries, and a workforce of more than 150,000. Gap eventually pitched out brands like Levi's and now sells only its own. It also evolved into a corporate behemoth that has acquired a group of once-funky stores that sold army surplus clothing called Banana Republic; launched Old Navy, a chain of discount stores with prices low enough that parents can buy clothing by the armful; created Forth & Towne, which briefly sold clothes for middle-aged women; and started a website to sell shoes called Piperlime. Gap's combined revenue is second only to Wal-Mart in terms of U.S. clothing sales. Though Gap is publicly traded, the founders and their children own 37 percent of the stock and are billionaires. While I was there, the CEO of Gap was Paul Pressler, who previously ran Disney's theme parks division. In orientation I was told to expect a visit from founders Don and Doris, who like to prowl around the stores without announcement or introduction.

But on my first day, such a connection to headquarters was not tangible. Alberto introduced me to some of my coworkers. There was Alfred, a slight Malaysian guy with a welcoming smile; Sam, a sweet Filipino man with his hair pulled back into a small ponytail; and Mark, just 21, who was heavyset, had a patchy beard, and wore three plastic cause-related bracelets. Alberto showed me how to use a walkie-talkie to call in a stock check to the stockroom in the basement, something we did whenever a customer couldn't find a size or color.

At first, wandering the sales floor, I had no idea where to find specific articles of clothing. Over time, however, the room sorted itself into sections: the office rotunda loaded with walls of khakis and office-casual attire, the undergarment area behind the register, the vintage jeans section that harked back to Gap's glory days, and the tables of multicolored T-shirts. These were sections I would learn well as I spent long stretches of time returning "go-backs" from the changing room to the sales floor. When not doing this, I folded clothes that needed to be folded; there was an endless supply created by our customers. Because I'm someone who needs more quantifiable and meaningful signs of achievement, walking around looking for stacks of shirts to refold neither came naturally to me nor satisfied me. I'm usually one who excels at hard, repetitive tasks, but there was something ridiculous about constantly folding shirts that were constantly being unfolded. On my first day, I had a gnawing sense of not really knowing what to do, but I received constant advice that I needed to be doing something. "A little secret," said one coworker. "Don't stand around, or management will say, 'Why isn't he doing anything?'" My first day was a blessedly abbreviated four-hour tour of duty; I wandered around aimlessly and tried to avoid both the eyes of my managers and the questions of customers before I was set free.

On the second afternoon, Alberto sent me downstairs to watch some training DVDs. Downstairs was the operations center for our store. A high-ceilinged basement patrolled by stockroom workers folding large swaths of clothes on broad tables, it was like a rabbit's warren of activity. Any stock not yet on the sales floors was stacked on ten-foot-high shelves that slid back and forth on metal tracks. The snack room and lockers and the time clock where we marked our comings and goings were all down there. Also there, behind the

scenes, was a video-monitoring room that afforded eyes all over the
store—managers could keep an eye on those of us on the sales floor
without actually being there, and loss-prevention teams scanned the
live feeds for theft in progress.

Alberto could not find the exact DVDs he was looking for, so
he put in a monthly managerial video report. A corporate executive delivered his message from the floor of a Gap store with an
overarching point that in its 35th year Gap was working on "reclaiming its equity in denim." Another DVD about customer service said, "The point is to just be friendly and helpful." It seemed
like a clear call to action, but I doubted my job would be so
simple.

On the wall was a chart that laid out the progression of new employees and described four kinds of workers along a spectrum of
training and indoctrination: There were "enthusiastic beginners"
(like me) who were "highly excited" and "don't know what they
don't know." There were "disillusioned learners" who were "stumbling on fundamental skills and losing energy." Then there were
"frustrated workers" with "competent skills bases" who were "not
seeing immediate results" and, at the top of the heap, "competent
individuals" who were "able to empower others." This was a less-
than-ideal workforce, with the only quality workers found at the
end of a troubling stretch of learning and disillusionment.

Each of our shifts began with what they called a "one minute," a
quick meeting with the on-floor manager in which we examined a
small printed spreadsheet. We looked at the sales goal for the day
and how the previous day measured up. The spreadsheet might
show a $40,000 goal for the men's department for the day ahead
and that sales were down 12 percent from the day-before goal. It
showed the average transaction per customer (which usually hov-
ered at 2.45 garments), as well as the "conversion rate" (the percent-
age of customers who entered the store and purchased something).

For a new guy like me, these numbers meant little, mostly because I had no effect on them.

After just three days on the job, I began to dread punching in. Something about the boredom of the job made me incredibly hungry. I was not sure I had ever experienced such hunger without exerting myself. At my breaks I polished off submarine sandwiches, sometimes three in an eight-hour shift. I started to bring PowerBars and packets of GU, a carbohydrate gel concoction that I usually ate when running long distances. I snuck to the bathroom to wolf the stuff down.

Most of the time we were, of course, folding clothes. That was what we did. Days went by during which it seemed as if I did nothing but fold clothes, and that was probably because that was just about all I did. The job was incredibly, absolutely, totally, astonishingly boring. My two daily assignments were (1) wandering around folding (or "touching up") and occasionally helping customers and (2) staffing the fitting room, seven small rooms in the corner of our sales floor. The fitting-room assignment was the real killer, because of the long stretches of time during which absolutely nothing occurred at all. It felt as if I were being forced to encounter a vacuum in time and space, retail limbo. There was nowhere to sit in the fitting room, and I was told more than once to wander outside the fitting room and touch up the sweaters when nobody was in the fitting rooms. According to the company, "The fitting room is the easiest place during the customers' shopping experience to add on. This is your chance to be the style expert. It is your role to make merchandise suggestions and show the customer how to wear key styles to create multiple outfits and wardrobes." But in reality, the fitting room was a sad corner of the store, overlooked by the store layout planners and not a place where customers could feel excited to expand their wardrobes.

Because Gap workers have to fold clothes only when customers make them messy, presumably we might vent our frustrations at any customers who, in essence, mess up our work—the *unfolders*. I never got there, but I did start to take issue with some inconsiderate customers. One day when I was running the fitting room, I allowed a slender guy with a messy beard in with a dozen garments. After trying them on, he left a pile of clothing six inches deep that I had to pick up and refold. I quickly learned to enforce the three-garment limit. The fitting room was usually uneventful, but one day I helped a color-blind couple to identify which clothes looked good together. Another day I watched as two girls and a guy friend laughed hysterically as he tried on outfits for a last-minute Halloween costume.

I tried, largely in vain, to do things to make the time go by. I counted how many items of clothing I folded each day. (One day it was 300 garments; the next it was 270.) I acted the part of a shopper and looked around for clothes that I might buy and found myself on more intimate terms with a line of clothing than I had ever been. The in-store displays convinced me to purchase more than one article of clothing that I would never wear.

Sure enough, I was rapidly moving into the phase of *disillusioned learner*: Knowledge is power, and I was learning next to nothing. One day I had what passed for an on-the-job epiphany. All of the merchandise was presented in such a way that customers could easily help themselves, grab clothes, and try them on. More than in other stores, clothing in Gap stores was laid out on tables instead of hung on hangers. *What Gap needs*, I thought to myself, *is an army of low-paid employees who are fairly presentable and all wear Gap clothes. They wander around folding because customers constantly unfold the merchandise. What Gap needs is an army of folders.* Then the thought fell apart as it dawned on me: I was a lowly member of this army of folders.

Paco Underhill, author of *Why We Buy*, runs a company that studies and perfects retail environments, including Gap, by using techniques such as shadowing consumers and noting just what they look at and touch, and for how long. He describes Gap as a place with a merchandising policy that "determines how and where employees spend their time [and which] translates into the need for lots of clerks roaming the floor rather than standing behind the counter ringing up sales. Which is a big expense." I was living out this merchandising policy: expensive for Gap but also unsatisfying for the employees.

While working at Gap I happened to be reading *The Long Walk*, the memoir of a Polish soldier captured by Russian troops in World War II who was sentenced to 35 years in a Siberian work camp and successfully escaped and walked to India. Gap was my gulag. I was constantly waiting for the end of the shift and counting time. This was especially true toward the end of an eight-hour shift, when I examined time in space-bending minute and half-minute increments. There were more parallels between *The Long Walk* and my new daily routine, including the feeling that one was always being watched by a range of eyes: security, management, and coworkers. I half expected my coworkers to say, "Hey, Alexi, what are you in for, comrade?"

Talking to coworkers was the best way to pass the time. Tom had messy blond hair in a loose bowl cut and slightly jumbled teeth, and he wore clothes that were a touch more wrinkled than others'. Tom, our resident philosopher, set me straight on the products we were selling. "Levi's 501s are made to go to the moon and shit," he told me. "Gap quality is a whole different story." He filled me in on the importance of eating regional, indigenous honey as a way to stay healthy: "If you live in Northern California, you need to eat honey collected in Northern California," he told me. "If I get a sore throat, the first thing I am going to do is find some locally harvested honey." A vegan, he launched into a discourse one day in the break room to educate a few of us on the perils of drinking milk: "Did you ever stop and wonder why humans are the only mammalian species of lifelong milk drinkers?" he asked us. "No other species drink other species' milk, so why should we?" He said he had come to work at Gap to try to work his way into the corporate offices down the street, hoping to be trained as a khaki specialist. Tom had a vivid four-inch blue bar code tattooed on the back of his neck. "A lot of people get tattoos at important moments in their lives," he told me one day as we folded khakis, but he never finished the thought.

Over time I got to know my other coworkers as we folded and talked. Pauliño moved from Brazil six months before and used to work at a coffee shop. Troy was living at home "temporarily." Reggie was newly arrived from Texas and a freshman at the San Francisco Academy of Art. He wore exclusively cargo pants and polo shirts. Luke sported the baggiest pants in the store and usually wore red Timberland boots and an untucked but ironed button-down shirt.

The rotunda was the only room on the men's floor with a window, a small aperture into the outside world where the sun rose and fell. The room was a round space stocked with the bulk of our office-casual attire. One day Troy and I were assigned to the rotunda, where we could talk and fold in peace, thanks to our distance from the floor's central hub of cash registers.

"Much of what is at the heart of a culture will not be revealed in the rules of behaviors taught to newcomers," writes corporate culture expert Edgar Schein. "It will only be revealed to members as they gain permanent status and are allowed to enter the inner circles of the group, where group secrets are shared." And so it was that Troy filled me in on the realities of Gap, in contrast to the airbrushed stuff they'd told us in orientation. He told me how Moses, our department's denim specialist, had started just a year before and had cranked his way to the top. He told me how, during the preholiday period, the store hired a ton of people and then gave them all few or no hours once the new year rolled around.

"When's your break?" he asked.

"I already had it," I said.

"Bummer," he said. "Dude, this place fucks with time. It slows down, it crawls, it moves backward."

One day toward the end of an eight-hour shift I was linked up with Sammy, a slim Asian guy in his early twenties who I had noticed was a hard worker. At the end of each day, our customers had rummaged through the clothes and left them on the floor, folded halfway on shelves, mixed with other nonmatching garments, pulled off hangers, and otherwise a mess. In addition to folding all day, we had to make a concerted effort at the end of the day to clean the store and fold each evening. I worked with Sammy to prepare the denim wall for the store close. Sunday was the day of the "perfect close," when each item had to be flawlessly folded or hung on a hanger in anticipation of a possible walk-through by executives from our corporate office. I heard about coworkers clocking in at 11 PM and then staying all night to do nothing but fold perfectly. But this was Friday night, so the folding didn't have to be perfect.

"This is the denim wall," Sammy told me, motioning to a wall of jeans. "This is where we put most of our denim, and before closing we have to get this wall in order." Sammy knew that I was new, so we started with the basics: He showed me the proper technique to fold a pair of blue jeans in a way that was quite different from how I had ever folded my own pants. Sammy showed me the "air-fold": the folding of a pair of jeans without use of a folding cart. To properly air-fold a pair of pants, you held the pants with the zipper (or button fly) facing you. Then you closed the pants like a book, with the zipper moving inward. You tucked the extra crotch fabric, or rise, under and took the bottom cuffs and folded them upward until the cuffs sat on the top of the left back pocket. Your last move was to tuck the legs once again under so that you were looking at the right back pocket and tag and a folded square-shaped pair of pants.

The denim wall was more than 30 feet across and had seven shelves top to bottom that held the bulk of our denim inventory. As I started to massage the wall into shape, more than one coworker stopped by to tell me I was lucky to be closing with Sammy, not the supercontrolling Moses. It was clear to me that informal training by coworkers might overshadow any official training modules I would be exposed to.

Getting the denim wall in order started with sizing, so that all of the washes (colors of blue) and all cuts of jeans were separated and the sizes moved from smallest (waist 28 inches, length 28 inches) to the largest (waist 46 inches, length 38 inches). When you had all pants folded and stacked in ascending order, you scrunched each six or seven pairs of stacked pants so that the stack assumed a semi-messy look, like a heartbeat represented on an EKG screen. Your goal was just the right semi-misshapen clump, according to Sammy, that would invite customers to approach and interact with the merchandise. If they saw a too-perfectly folded stack, they might feel that they weren't allowed to touch them, so a scrunch was an invitation to touch. To properly scrunch, you not only squeezed the front of the stack but also reached back and scrunched the entire stack; otherwise, you ended up with a scrunch that didn't stay scrunched. It was harder and more time-consuming than it seemed it would be, and my fingers were soon tired. (Later I found out that not all Gap stores scrunch their jeans.) After I folded and scrunched a couple of rows, Sammy came over and pulled out a few improperly shelved pants. Though I would soon be able to tell a "whiskered authentic" wash (which creates fake creases in the crotch area) from a "sandblasted vintage" with a quick glance, at this early stage such differences remained imperceptible to me.

After an hour spent at the wall going through these steps, I asked Sammy to check out my work. He had a few minor adjustments to make but overall was complimentary. "The wall looks okay," Sammy told me, "but watch out when you work with Moses. He's hardcore. He's hella picky." Sammy described how Moses approached a wall you had just sized, stacked, folded, and scrunched, and said casually, "Which one is out of place?" He then left you to find the errant pair of jeans, say the boot-cut mistakenly slotted in the straight-cut stack. In addition to being a denim specialist, Moses was an elevated sales coach, a position two steps below the department manager. Employees who worked for some length of time were encouraged to choose specialties—in areas such as denim or khaki—and after a day of off-site training they returned to the store as in-house specialists. A specialist also taught new people like me and worked with the visuals team that placed the clothes on in-store mannequins and hung jumbo-size photographs high on our walls. Having specialists inspired the staff to learn and built in a level of respect for coworkers' authority regarding a product type. Instead of building a culture of generalists, Gap built micro-experts.

When I was eventually paired with Moses for denim training, I expected to meet a large older guy, a Zen monk of denim, but instead found an energetic and focused, if hung over, college kid. Moses was just shy of six feet tall and had black hair spiked with visible gel. He wore a loose-fitting black polo shirt and a pair of straight-leg pants with a boot cut that flared slightly around his shoes. He was in his third year of college. He seemed to cherish each pair of Gap denim we stocked. The jeans, it seemed, were not Gap's property but his own. He was militant in his upholding of standards in the denim department.

The first thing we did at the denim wall was to select one or two pairs of each of the jean cuts (loose straight, straight cut, loose boot cut, and boot cut) in my size. Moses had me try on each of the pairs and stand before the multiple-angle mirror and describe what I saw as specific to each cut. It was a rare opportunity for an employee to experience being a customer, and a smart way to indoctrinate green employees like me. I needed some new jeans anyway—under Gap rules, I could not wear any jeans with the stitching of a competitor. Gap had created ways for customers to easily understand product lines by creating its own broad, easily identifiable categories so choices that might bewilder customers were rendered simple. Customers who didn't have the time or inclination to familiarize themselves with particulars were given basic choices within which to decide, and we, the employees, were taught how to guide them there.

As I put on one pair after another, Moses helped me to identify what made each cut different. I'd vaguely taken notice that jeans had undergone a bit of reworking in recent years, but I had not paid attention to specifics. I used the fitting to probe my own comfort level with the now-popular looser styles. While I was mostly wearing the basic, iconic, original Levi's 501 riveted, five-pocket, button-fly jeans (supposedly the best-selling garment of all time), jeans in the past decade had been modified; they had been stone-washed, acid-washed, ripped, torn, ozonated, and distressed with a slew of caustic enzymes and chemicals. Once the indestructible go-to pants of the gold miner, now jeans were meant to be turned inside out, washed in cold water, and air-dried like silk blouses.

If Gap was indeed "reclaiming its equity in denim," then this very denim wall in our store was a shrine to the reclamation. Our 37,000-square-foot store was the flagship (the leading store within a company that is usually the biggest in size and stock holding, and used as a benchmark against which other stores are measured; they are typically in conspicuous shopping areas and can shape local buying habits), so Moses was, in essence, the keeper of the brand. If *reclaiming* was the buzzword, it meant equity had been lost. But Moses was the person to reclaim it, to recover it, seize it, and promote it. For us, reclaiming such an equity meant convincing customers to buy a lot of jeans.

I proudly told Moses what I had done the day before. I had found a customer hovering in front of the denim wall. I had eagerly approached this customer and described each cut to him, asked him his size, and then sent him into the changing room loaded with a fat stack of jeans. There, I imagined, he would try them all on and see what he liked. This, according to Moses, was precisely the wrong approach. Moses explained that this customer most surely exited the changing room far more confused than when he entered it. You could not count on the customer to be very invested in identifying the right cut for himself and understanding the nuances of our tailoring. With my approach, the customer would wind up perplexed and befuddled and roll out of the store leaving a pile of denim on the changing room floor.

Moses taught me a few rules of thumb about sizing and picking out the right pair for a customer. He taught me the "four Ws": whom you are shopping for; what size, style, or color you are looking for; where you will use them; and when you will need them. The best way to identify what a customer would want to purchase, he said, was by looking at what he was wearing when he walked in. Almost all European tourists, whom we saw a lot of in San Francisco, wanted straight jeans with tapered ankles. You pulled out the straight-cut pants for these customers. If a kid walked in with sagging jeans three sizes too large, you sent him over to the rack of our widest-cut jeans, which Moses called the Lewis Slouch.

As we worked together, I felt increasingly inferior to Moses—he had boundless knowledge and passion for the products he sold, and I was a study in cluelessness. He was the *competent individual* and I was the *enthusiastic beginner* quickly evolving into a *disillusioned learner*. He was a true fan of Gap brand and told me he owned more than a dozen pairs of jeans. He wore them well too—belted low enough so the cuffs broke right on his shoelaces.

Moses reflected on the vagaries of identifying your own perfect pair of jeans. While we were in the dressing room he delivered an inspired and enthusiastic soliloquy, an ode to blue jeans: "Everyone has a pair of jeans that makes them feel awesome, feel right. Everyone's got one pair of jeans that fit well and inspire confidence when they wear them. It's the pair that makes you feel like *you are the man*. For me it's my pair of Gap Worker jeans that I can wear into a bar and walk up to, like, any girl and feel totally confident. I can go to a job interview and rock it. You have a pair of jeans that you love, right?" he said, pointing directly at me. And he was right; the pair has changed over the years, but there's always one pair that rises to the top of my stack of pants.

What makes that pair of pants *that pair of pants* is a long equation that involves current fashion; how you feel about yourself; whether a pair is wrinkled or smooth, dark, or light; how the cuff breaks; and whether the pants have enough or not enough distress. Our job, presumably, was to help our customers find *that pair of pants*. Gap would live or die on the basis of how many of its customers felt at least some part of this connection to their trousers.

Lately, Gap had been more dead than alive. Gap was in the news a lot while I was working at the store in 2005. The just-ended quarter marked the worst sales for Gap in three years, with profits tumbling 20 percent and sales down 3 percent from the previous year. The press had taken notice of Gap's stagnant stock price. Analysts were weighing in with various theories for the retailer's lackluster sales. One said customers were too confused by the merchandise. One said he'd seen only one chain (JCPenney) shake an extended slump like Gap's. Another said that when frustrated shoppers change their buying habits, they tend to stay changed. "Without a defining product vision, Gap is unlikely to be the cultural presence it once was," said one article.

At the time, it seemed possible that Gap, once one of the world's most effective mass-market design engines that spawned "office casual" and the American uniform of the late twentieth century, had stopped producing anything innovative or noteworthy. Gap's CEO, Paul Pressler, was perceived as being good at "metrics" (crunching numbers) but not fashion, unlike former CEO Mickey Drexler. Some criticized the company for being led by a team, not a charismatic leader. At the same time, the press went along with Gap's excitement over what it called the "Denver concept," a new store design that included dark wood floors, coffee tables covered with magazines, softer lighting, and spacious fitting rooms. (Months later, when I went to Denver to investigate the new stores, I found them unworthy of any sort of hope. Designers, no doubt controlled by committee, had merely changed small things such as the color of flooring and not gone forward with any comprehensive alterations.)

The blame for Gap's demise might have been pinned on the clothing designers and trend forecasters at the company who seemed to have lost touch with design and fashion and Gap's customer base. Gap's bread and butter, khakis and denim, no longer came in many new form-fitting cuts, the stores recycled decades-old fashions and fabrics, and no amount of national advertising seemed to be able to convince customers that Gap clothing was fresh, not stale. According to retail experts, retail stores have three distinct aspects that work together to move product: the premises, whatever you put in them, and what employees do. From what I could tell, Gap was intent on changing the store design first, then the clothes. Perhaps the employees would then follow.

Before denim training was over, Moses imparted another rule of thumb for sizing. If we don't have someone's size, he said, you could use a simple mathematical equation to offer them another pair to try on. "I love math; that's why I am a math major," he said. "Let's say a customer is a 32 by 34, but we don't have that size in stock. You add an inch to the waist and subtract two inches from the length," said Moses. "So what's the next pair you are going to have this guy try on?"

"A 33 by 32," I told him.

"Good. So what's that equation again?"

As for Moses, they should have bottled his enthusiasm and spread it around Gap headquarters. They should have filmed this man in action and put him into Gap TV ads as GapMan. If you looked at Gap's year-over-year sales figures, they were flat. The company was like a sinking ship. Forget changing the store design and adding new cuts of jeans—employees like Moses were Gap's only hope of salvation.

One day I was talking with Alberto when our floor manager, Joaquin, walked by and simply pointed at Alberto's feet and wagged his finger. We weren't allowed to wear sport shoes on the sales floor. Gap's dress code decreed that we wear either Gap-brand clothes or clothes that didn't bear any markings of competitive brands. Though he should have known better, Alberto had the look of a kid caught trying to get away with something, and he grudgingly walked to his basement locker to change out of his Nikes.

Clothing your employees in the clothes you sell is not a new idea; the goal is to create a universe in which employees show what the clothes look like on actual people. Treating the employees as live mannequins is called wardrobing by the industry. Clothes are constantly changing, and for most retailers it is too costly to provide free clothes to employees every season. Instead, many clothing companies issue guidelines, or dress codes, to instill uniformity. Such dress codes are a tricky practice that at Gap came to a head in 2004. Dress codes, like just about everything in modern American workplaces, are heavily regulated and governed by state and federal laws. As a result, labor lawyers are quick to level class-action lawsuits for perceived infractions.

In 2004, when Robert Boleyn worked at a Gap store in Hollywood, California, he found the dress code to be overbearing. He claimed that managers required him to buy and wear Gap clothes, and that he was spending a lot of his weekly paycheck on clothing to wear to work. Boleyn found that in practice his managers criticized employees who wore non-Gap clothing. Boleyn got in touch with Patrick Kitchin, a San Francisco lawyer who had become something of an expert on employee dress codes, having filed suit against Polo Ralph Lauren for a policy he alleged violated the State of California's Unfair Competition Law. Kitchin filed a suit against Gap. In response, Gap said its written policy simply required employees to look "brand-appropriate" and wear Gap-like clothing that didn't bear a competitor's brand name.

In California (and a dozen other states with similar statutes), there is a gray area that surrounds the issue of dress codes versus uniforms. California law prohibits companies from requiring workers to pay for uniforms as a condition of employment. Places such as Polo, Chico's, and Gap (all of which Kitchin filed lawsuits against) say that they have dress codes, not uniform policies. The critical distinction, according to the law, is that the term *uniform* "includes wearing apparel and accessories of distinctive design or color." Kitchin argued that if you require employees to wear name-brand clothing (such as Gap or Polo), you are requiring an employee to wear distinctive apparel, and thus a uniform. Kitchin went on to settle the lawsuit with Gap on behalf of Boleyn and 55,000 current and former Gap workers in an agreement that awarded $1.4 million in Gap gift cards to workers (in amounts of $50 to $260) and $400,000 in attorney's fees but did not, in fact, force Gap to alter its policy. Certainly when I worked there, I could perceive no major change.

AT GAP WE often took our breaks down in the basement in a small snack room with vending machines and lockers. The basement was mostly populated by a serious army of folders and stock minders and a cranking boom box. When I did leave the building for a 15-minute break, coming and going ate up half the time. One day I walked out our customer entrance to save time and was upbraided by a manager on the way in. Because of security concerns, we were not allowed to use those doors at all. One afternoon after a break, I walked through the basement with David, the guy who hired me. The boom box in the center of the stock room blasted rapper Jay-Z: "*I moved from Levi's to Guess to Versace, now it's diamonds like Liberace.*"

David paused, stepped over to the CD player, and turned it way down. "If anyone asks who turned this down," he said to a guy standing nearby, "you can tell them that it was me." We got in the elevator to head up to the second floor. "We can't play that kind of music. We can't play it in the basement for the same reason we would not play it in the store: It's vulgar and offensive and it could make someone feel threatened about their workplace."

David and I rode in the elevator together and got off on the second floor, where the music was about as far from Jay-Z as possible. On the sales floor, music constantly played in the background, but it was carefully constructed audio branding. Songs we heard on the floor had been selected by an audio programmer who worked for Muzak, based in Fort Mill, South Carolina, one of the two major audio programming firms. (Some one million people hear Muzak music each day.) On the sales floor we were not so much listening to music as having it broadcast at us, and in tight, recurring loops as short as 12 songs in length. Until 1983, Gap stores played the radio; now audio tracks the limited songs in rotation at Top 40 stations. Like corporate-controlled radio, Gap tries to be all things to all customers.

Alvin Collis, former senior vice president of strategy and brand at Muzak, told me that music in a retail store is not entertainment at all but a vessel to carry emotion. He said the societal shift away from utilitarian purchases had led to widespread changes in in-store environments. "Retail has a problem: Nobody needs to buy anything anymore. Because we don't need anything, the entire driver to get people to buy things is gone. What we buy now is no longer based on needs but on how we want to portray ourselves in the world." Accordingly, retail must now be an experience for customers, and Collis sees retail as theater. "You build a theater, which is the store," he said, "then you hire the actors, who are sales associates, and you give them all costumes. And then every day you put on a show."

Companies such as Muzak take a brand such as Gap and find music that relates to what the brand is trying to accomplish in the marketplace through a specific "brand personality." It's all about customization of atmosphere through music. At Gap the goal is a soundtrack that makes its wide range of customers all feel welcome.

According to Jeff Daniel, president of Rock River Music, which sells branded CD mixes to major retailers including Gap, "public sound" has different duties depending on the retailer. At Starbucks, the approach to music is to play both retro music that appeals nostalgically to customers while also introducing them to new music that can be purchased. The guiding principle at Starbucks, says

Daniel, is "You are busy. You stopped following new music after college. You no longer have time to keep track of it, so we will take care of it for you." In the hip cosmetic boutique Sephora, on the other hand, the music is chosen to create an atmosphere of aspiration. At youth clothing outfitter Abercrombie & Fitch, the idea is to play new rock and hip-hop so loud that it chases away older people and leaves the store filled with young faces. At Gap the goal is to reach a wider audience and offend nobody—except those of us working there.

In our store the music was a tiring, painfully repetitive loop of the same dozen songs carefully chosen to lubricate shopping for the lowest common denominator of shopper. My coworkers confirmed that the same music, in tight rotation, played for six to eight weeks. To me it came to feel like audio water torture, with simple choruses popping occasionally into focus: "It's not the fall that hurts, it's when you hit the ground. I just want . . . something for nothing. I want to love somebody." Once the store closed at 9 PM, the music was turned down or completely off. "My whole body changes," my coworker Raoul said to me. "It's like my whole body relaxes when the music goes off." Raoul, a short man of maybe 19, wore his brown hair in a mop top. He often wore a tight argyle V-neck sweater with a plaid shirt underneath and khakis pegged at the ankles in a mod fashion. He had created his own anti-Gap fashion statement, an original nouveau-preppy look that both celebrated and mocked Gap's design heritage. Raoul also worked at Borders, sometimes pulling back-to-back seven-hour shifts. He said he was piling up cash by working 70 hours a week but didn't really know what the point was.

Outside the store was the tourist-packed cable car turnaround on bustling Market Street, where tourists mixed with locals hanging around the broad-shouldered street corner, darting around the sidewalk acting wild or sitting at folding tables playing chess. This boulevard was one of San Francisco's more hospitable areas to the wayward and homeless, who at times filtered into our store. One guy I saw inside quite often was a tall, crazy-eyed man dressed in what looked like the faded blue uniform of a Confederate soldier. He wore a ukulele strapped with fishing line around his neck and followed me through the store saying he needed to show my business card to someone at Homeland Security.

The in-house term for disreputable customers was NORs (for "no receipts"). They were the people who returned most likely stolen merchandise in the hope of getting cash. With no receipt, we could issue only a store credit, and NORs were typically unhappy about this. Some came in with expired identification cards and got belligerent. Others staged elaborate attempts to convince the employees at the register that they were bona fide shoppers by bringing in large groups of family members. It was a time-worn charade.

Other sketchy characters in our store were in fact Gap employees—but it took me a few days to figure that out. One day I saw a tall man with curly brown hair lurking around the sales floor and I asked him if he needed help, just as we were shown in orientation. He did not reply. Then a few days later I found myself sitting next to him in the snack room and realized that he worked for Loss Prevention, or LP—he was one of our in-house undercover cops. And he was not alone. I started to connect the dots, recognizing the shadily dressed guys who popped up regularly on our floor. My favorite of these guys was Ted Chan, a short guy who seemed to take his job seriously while also having fun. He walked around the floor and tried on clothing. He interacted with the merchandise. One morning he vamped for a full 10 minutes in front of a mirror trying on a succession of newly arrived striped winter scarves, no doubt for the entertainment of his fellow basement-dwelling video-monitoring crew. Whenever LP identified potentially criminal activity, they dispatched their troops like special ops teams to covertly stake out our sales floor. There was no doubt about it; they had the best job in the store.

Strangely, the first thing I learned at my four-hour Gap orientation was about theft. My group watched a DVD titled *Risky Business* that included grainy imagery labeled "real store footage" that showed an old woman clearing off a rack of underwear into an open bag, another woman stuffing her bag full of shirts, and a young mother tucking garments into a baby carriage. We watched reenactments showing thieves skulking into dark, unwatched corners of the store. We learned that thieves stick to well-known patterns, such as working in groups of three, with one member who distracts while the others steal. We were told that regular employees are not allowed to intercept or apprehend suspected thieves; that was the role of the loss-prevention staff. We were taught that the best way to prevent shoplifting was with great customer service, and we were encouraged to use "recovery statements" to deter thefts: When you saw a customer bundle away a blue T-shirt, you might ask him if he wanted to try a yellow one. We were told that employees steal more than the thieves who come into the store. The DVD showed a former Gap worker in eerie silhouette saying he stole freely for three weeks, unaware he was under surveillance. "Gap is smart," he concluded, and we all laughed.

Just a mile from worldwide corporate headquarters, our store was the flagship of flagships, and Tom, the vegan philosopher, told me that the CEO had decided to "make our store his own little project," though I was not sure what exactly that meant. Tom told me that the CEO was a real "T-shirts and jeans sort of guy."

One afternoon I was straightening hangers and clothes on the messy rack where we put the most marked-down garments in the far back of our sales floor when my coworker Troy joined me. "Hey, did you hear that a regional director or some sort of manager, maybe he's a vice president or something—some serious dude—is in our store? He's in here. Everybody's, like, getting ready for him. . . . Oh, there he is over there in that yellow sweater."

I gazed across to the table of shirts, and sure enough, there was a guy in a yellow sweater. I knew his face from Gap's annual report, from the stippled illustration in a recent copy of the *Wall Street Journal*, and the welcome DVD we all watched in orientation. He was Paul Pressler, the CEO—our boss. Technically he was our leader, but the chain of command was so lengthy that it was as if we worked for two companies, one the place of ideas, the other the place of folding. He wore a white T-shirt underneath a yellow wool sweater and blue jeans with a faint wash. It was a Saturday afternoon and he appeared to be floating around inspecting the store in action, exploring the gritty reality outside the hermetically sealed corporate headquarters.

Probably because of his high rank—he was at the top and I was at the bottom—my pulse quickened with this ridiculous thought: *He knows that I know that he knows that I'm an undercover reporter. And he might have something to say to me that I won't be able to answer.*

There he was, folding a black merino sweater that was on sale. Then he was taking an errant hanger back to the register area. I was frozen for a second. Then I thought that he must have thought that we didn't know who he was, that he could travel somewhat anonymously in our ranks. He had no entourage. It was his plan we were carrying out. He was the commander in chief and we were the grunts on the front lines. He had waded into the trenches to help us in the battle. Or had he? I could not decide if he was trying to help out or to send a message that we were not doing our job. Gap exists because of the vision he articulated and broadcast to those of us on the front lines. He was closing the loop and we were carrying out his vision with our every move. (My yearly salary would be less than $15,000; his was $1.7 million in cash and more in stock options.) I felt naked and sure that he would confront me. Instead, my coworker Lee approached him with a broad smile. Lee was a very effeminate short guy who wore a flower behind his ear and painted his finger- and toenails, wore dark mascara and flip-flops, and had a bleached-blond Mohawk—all of which seemed that they must violate Gap dress code. Lee engaged the CEO briefly in conversation, and then the CEO was gone.

Apparently a number of employees from headquarters, not only the CEO, often wandered around our store, taking notice of what they saw. One letter I saw tacked up on a bulletin board in the basement lauded every department but men's. The letter writer made note of a lunch break spent strolling around our store acting the part of a shopper. To her, the women's and baby sections seemed like great examples of departments that had turned around in recent months. But when she walked through our department, nobody greeted her, there was no effort by my crew to engage her, and she was not pleased.

In the first few days at Gap I was taught by a young advanced sales coach named Gabriela, who went to school all morning and showed up for work in the midafternoon. She told me that she grew up on the Mexico–United States border in El Paso and was a first-generation American. She wore tight pants, a pair of slip-on Chinese black slippers, a tight-fitting maroon blouse, and a belt studded like a dog collar. Like a lot of my men's department co-workers, Gabriela talked about how our department was the best in the store and had a real sense of community. Gabriela said, "They are still trying to figure out morale issues on other floors." It was a buoying sentiment I heard often enough to make me change my own behavior as I tried to help the team stay on top.

Gabriela taught me about GapCards and customer service. She told me that once you had had even the smallest interaction with a customer, you had built a "mini-relationship" with that person, and because of this tenuous bond, he or she would later seek you out. When she said "mini-relationship," she threw up air quotes in a way I saw a lot in training at Gap and other retailers. It was a quick way to let your coworker know that you might be teaching the company's lessons but that you still stood outside, that you hadn't swallowed everything whole without some independent thought. Gabriela explained that to establish these mini-relationships, you might simply ask customers whether they had found what they were looking for, and they might say that they were all set. But five minutes later, they would hunt you down when they needed to find, say, a larger size for a particular Gap logo sweatshirt.

Sure enough, the next day I answered a quick question for a German customer about where he could find a pair of khakis. Ten minutes later, he came looking for me. We had developed a mini-relationship, just as Gabriela said we would. He had found a pair of black khakis that fit well, but we didn't have a pair of brown khakis in the same size, and he wanted to take advantage of the reduced price if he bought two pair of pants. He ended up walking the six blocks to another store, buying the brown pair and walking back to our store, where we processed the purchase and discount. I apologized for sending him on a 12-block errand, but he was not put out at all: "In Europe we like to walk a lot," he said.

A GAPCARD IS a credit card that allows customers who sign up for it to get an initial discount on their purchase and then other discounts in the future. For the company it's a way to act the part of a credit-card issuer and both save on paying credit-card fees and make money on those customers who incur finance charges. Apparently those who sign up for GapCards are twice as likely to shop at Gap again, and buy double the amount of goods that non-card-holders buy. If store credit cards were once a minor part of the retail clothing business, at Gap they were all-important. We even wore orange cards around our necks advertising these cards. Gabriela and I role-played just how to sell customers on signing up for a card and how to counter a range of customer objections, including "I have too many credit cards already" and "It won't save me much." I knew that I would not advance far unless I pushed my customers into signing up. In the basement there was a chart on which every sales clerk in the store was listed together with the number of Gap-Cards he or she had sold to customers. The chart showed each employee as a cut-out character with a name on it. The more cards you sold, the closer you got to a VIP room within an imaginary club, but right then most of us were out in the street, beyond the velvet rope. I had already heard about Ziggy, the newly promoted manager, who advanced mainly because of his ability to hustle. If my coworkers' stories were to be believed, he managed to sell an astonishing 106 cards in his first month on the job, less than a year before. He had been promoted, no doubt, as an example for the rest of us. Gabriela told me that as a store we were "goaled" at signing up 40 customers for GapCards each day.

A few days in, I was working away folding T-shirts when Moses, ever serious, approached me.

"Alex, can I have a word with you?" he asked.

"No problem," I said.

"Alex, as a store we are currently at 36 GapCards for the day. The men's department is at 14 out of 36; we are not carrying the store. We are underselling our own department from yesterday, and we are behind the rest of the departments in the store. I know we can do better. I need your help on this."

I told him I could help.

"Tell me, Alex," he said. "What are your true, true reservations about the GapCard?"

He pulled the truth, the real truth, right out of me. "I think they are a pain in the ass for the customers, and they really don't give them much of a discount. It's just a way for Gap to make money on money, and it's kind of a scam," I said.

True to form, Moses was ready to counter my true feelings by sharing with me some real value for these cards, and he did not even seem angry, though I was sure I had postponed any possible promotion by being so honest.

Toward the end of my time at Gap, my coworkers were quitting, dropping like flies. One day Alfred came in a little late—it turned out he'd just had his exit interview. When everyone asked, he said he was going "somewhere else." Another guy, Monty, was bailing out too, after what he said were years of on-and-off work at Gap. "I'm going to a better place" was all he would say. New to town, the Swedish company H&M was certainly poaching talent. My coworkers talked about a sign-on bonus they were offering that included airfare to New York. In fact, Gabriela told me that when another clothing store wanted to find good salespeople, they sent in fake customers to our store. If you did an exceptional job, they might give you their card and encourage you to call them. Attrition was in the air. I myself was bored, and there was little at Gap that made me excited to stay.

I had done what I'd hoped to do, to linger at Gap longer than I could as a customer. I came, I saw, I folded. I had crossed the line long enough to paint a picture for myself of a workplace filled with a variety of actors who played many roles as they collectively attempted to export Gap-designed costumes to a world that had grown less interested in what the company had to offer. The uniform of casual dress that had taken the world by storm two decades before was no longer in demand, and Gap had found no replacement for that company-defining product line. It was clear to me, working at Gap, that if the product a company sold was neither interesting nor compelling to consumers, then the company could do little to halt boredom, dejection, and lack of enthusiasm from swelling into the employee ranks.

My last shift ended on a Friday night. I was slated to work until 11, with two hours of folding following six hours in the fitting room. The music went off in our department and we began to fold. I tackled a long line of T-shirts hung on hangers. There were probably 200, and after a day of fondling by customers they sloped left and right. It took a long time to bring them all into conformity. Then I moved on to refolding all the sweaters stacked on several tables. One manager was on duty and made a few announcements over the public-address system. Apparently Pauliño, on my floor, had unplugged the scent-emitting machine, so the manager scolded us, telling us we could not do that again. I hadn't been aware that the store was artificially scented, but I saluted Pauliño's act of insubordination. I felt a magnetic pull to the elevator, wanting to bail out before my shift was over, to escape the gulag at long last. And miraculously, the manager on duty released the entire store at 10:15. He walked by us, gesticulating toward the elevator. "You guys have done great. Go, go, go!" We took the elevator downstairs and a line formed as we exited. Each of our bags was searched by Loss Prevention as we filed out into the dark night.

FIVE

GET BIG, STAY SMALL

When I walked into Starbucks on my first day, I caught the eye of Marty, the store manager, who was behind the counter pouring hot water over coffee grounds in an eight-cup stainless-steel French press. He motioned for me to find a seat. Marty was in his mid-twenties and had buzzed blond hair and the traces of a slim beard lining his jaw. He wore khakis and a white linen shirt. We sat together in the middle of the café, among the afternoon customers. Marty decanted a cup of coffee for each of us and said that the brew was made from Ethiopian Sidamo beans. Marty coached me through the right way to sip coffee. He asked me what flavors I tasted and what scents I smelled. I had few words besides the obvious: *hot, aromatic, earthy*.

Marty detected hints of lemon, he told me, and explained the practice of planting lemon trees in Ethiopian coffee fields to shape aroma. This first day at Starbucks, an experience shared by all employees, is called "First Impressions." It is the equivalent of trying on the line of jeans at Gap, an introduction in well-trained hands, and I had a lot to learn.

The format of our meeting encouraged me to step back a few steps and think about coffee and its flavor differently. I breathed in the smells with new vigor and let the coffee career hotly through my mouth and down my throat. Marty produced a slice of lemon pound cake; the lemon flavors in the coffee, he said, accentuated the cake and made a good match. We were sharing a cup of coffee and reflecting on international coffee-harvesting techniques and food and beverage pairings. After the grueling training course at Enterprise Rent-A-Car and the mind-numbing tour of duty folding clothes at Gap, I could live with this for the next couple of months.

Marty asked me what the phrase *fair trade* meant to me; I told him that it had something to do with coffee grown in a labor-friendly way. Marty asked me what the name *Howard Schultz* meant to me; I told him that he was the chairman of Starbucks. He told me about Howard growing up in the projects in New York and his father getting hurt while his mother was pregnant with her fourth child and that his father worked for a company that did not have workers' compensation, so the family had trouble paying its bills. He told me: "This is why Howard Schultz cares so much about us, the partners."

Marty said I would hear a lot about Starbucks as a third place. "The first place is home, the second place is the office, and for many people, Starbucks is the third place: not home and not the office." He pointed to a customer. "Paul comes to our store almost every day, working on his laptop and his cell phone. Starbucks is Paul's third place." It sounded like our store might be more like Paul's *second place*, so I asked whether it was a problem that Paul sat all day even if he did not buy much.

"Would we ever ask him to leave?" I asked Marty.

"Absolutely not, never," he said.

Coffee. I'm a big fan of the beverage, even if I am not the most knowledgeable about how or where it is grown. Coffee works with my brain chemistry; it has a sneaky way of expanding my mental faculties, of broadening the thoughts I have, of brightening my mood and giving me flashes of illumination. Like many people, I feel the pull of a coffee shop where for a few dollars I can buy a cappuccino and get a quick break from my ordinary daily routine. I've stopped in for coffee in cafés and carts all over the world, and each experience is a way to connect with the local scene.

To most people, Starbucks represents something: For many it's simply a place to get a cup of coffee on the way to work; for others the chain's rapid global spread is indicative of a dark side of capitalism, the homogenization of cityscapes, and the spreading sameness of neighborhoods. Issues such as these are not foreign to the company. It is precisely the company's attempt to represent something that has piqued so much interest. The intent of Starbucks to be this "third place," not just a place for coffee and doughnuts, gets people riled up. Since the early-1990s, more than 500 Starbucks outlets had opened within a half-hour drive from my house. After applying at several, I got a job offer to work as a barista, a job imbued with mystique despite being so common. There's no doubt about it: Starbucks operates on a grand scale. The year I applied, the company had 130,000 employees and received 584,000 applications. I was excited to find out what Starbucks felt like from the other side of the counter, what it would be like to, in my mind, become a part of the problem, not the solution.

OUR STORE LOOKED like most Starbucks stores: two overstuffed chairs, a long counter with baked goods displayed in a refrigerated pastry case, an under-the-counter cooler filled with cold drinks, two cash registers, and two substantial silver Verismo 801 espresso machines. The large picture windows of our store looked on to San Francisco's Union Street. In operation for 13 years, the store was showing its age, and its pockmarked hardwood floors were encrusted with dirt and dried coffee.

Starbucks advertises its entry-level barista position as one for which no experience is required, so training is geared to teaching new employees everything they will need to do the job. The training manual is imposing, and there is much to learn. The first two days on the job I sat in the middle of the store and made my way through the thick spiral-bound employee *Learning Journey Guide*. At first I got a sense that the training would be productive. But training at Starbucks is set up around having a "learning coach," and I had been assigned no coach. The store's computer crashed halfway through my simulation cash register training. When I had a question, I badgered other partners. An assistant manager named Erika dropped by my table and very clearly explained many important things, such as the difference between mild and bold coffees (mild coffees are roasted less and have more caffeine). She would have been a great coach, but she had no time for me. One of my coworkers, Gonzalez, also stopped by: "Man, I never learned nothing from that book," he said. "I learned it all hands-on!" I asked another coworker, Nina, for help, but she blew me off, and then quit the next week. There were a lot of training materials, but my store was too fast-paced for me to properly digest the information. There seemed to be an understanding that we would each figure it out, and I was mostly on my own.

On my third day I wore a green apron and served my first shift behind the register. I felt underprepared to be in front of live customers, but I was fortunate to work during an afternoon, when we usually saw fewer customers than in the morning. And my coworkers were there to help me. Starbucks has crafted a culture of teamwork so that any individual partner can't fail alone but will instead be a weak link in a connected chain. The most unsettling thing about the position "on register," traditionally the first stop for new and inexperienced Starbucks employees, was that customers knew more about how to do my job than I did. Many were regulars, people who worked nearby. Some helpfully pointed me to certain buttons on the cash register when I searched for them, and others showed me how to extract funds from their Starbucks debit cards. Still, many were simply impatient at my slowness. Some long lines grew in front of my register as I hemmed and hawed. Though I was a brand-new employee, I was wearing no sign that identified me as such, and found myself apologizing for taking 20 to 30 seconds longer than I should.

I had a pretty good handle on the basics. I knew the unique Starbucks sizing system: a very small drink is a "short," a small is a "tall," a medium is a "grande," and a large is a "venti." This is the lingo that Starbucks has trained its customers to use. Some customers use none of the Starbucks terms; others use it in the wrong order. I had to mark orders on cups correctly to get customers the right drink, and I had to ring their orders up for the right amount; customers who misuse the Starbucks jargon could wreak havoc on a new employee like me.

As an occasional Starbucks customer, I had never adopted the language, but as an employee, I used it without irony. When the drink orders came flying in fast, I had to listen carefully:

Yeah, I'll have a double nonfat soy vanilla latte. . . . Give me a soy macchiato. No, make that a soy caramel macchiato. . . . A triple long extra pump white mocha, please. . . . I'll have my regular—a double tall sugar-free hazelnut latte. . . . Can I have an iced venti Americano? A tall Tazo chai tea latte? . . . A grande double espresso Frappuccino. . . . A cappuccino with caramel drizzle. . . . A triple no-foam latte.

On and on it went. The language is a sophisticated and successful method of building customer loyalty: If a customer feels ownership of a drink, he or she will be inclined to come back and order it day after day. It was a rare customer who ordered just a plain cup of coffee. Starbucks is all about "mass customization," about meeting customers' many individual preferences while maintaining low costs. To study the names for the many beverages, I was sent home with a set of dice stamped with different drinks and modifiers. One throw might yield "Tall/Mocha/Add Syrup/½ Caf," and another, "Single/Decaf/Extra Whip/Coffee." I had to make sense of the pieces and how they fit together in the proper hierarchy.

From the outside it looked like the job was tailor-made for slackers, but I was finding it less than easy. The amount of learning in the early weeks was immense, and things would get easier, but when you work at a busy store, you are a cog in a fast-moving machine. Though at a lot of non-Starbucks coffee shops the servers spend a good deal of time talking with customers, I rarely did. We always had something to do. It surprised me to find how taxing a job like this could be.

Our customers were as different as their drink orders. An emergency-room doctor dressed in scrubs and a white lab coat stopped by at dawn every day on the way to the hospital and always requested ice in his extra-large coffee. A man in his late seventies asked me if he could put on one of our disposable clear plastic pastry gloves to feel the springiness of the chocolate-chip cookies. "I can't hear too well. I can't see too well," said a very old woman, who had scraggly white hair bound with a chrome barrette. She said she liked our coffee very much. "Please tell me the name of the coffee today." I told her it was Yukon. One woman wanted me to fill two baby bottles with warm milk, for which I did not charge her. One regular customer cut through the lingo and ordered a small black coffee with "no room, no lid, no sleeve." A mother sent up her eight-year-old daughter to order her special drink, a "no-whip, extra-hot, one pump of caramel, one pump of chocolate mocha." The young girl glanced back at her mom to make sure she was saying it right and putting the extra dollar tip in the right place.

A customer in his mid-eighties, the picture of geriatric health, told me he had never seen a doctor in his life. Carol Doda, the first topless dancer to have her breasts injected with silicone and celebrated by Tom Wolfe in "The Put-Together Girl," owned a lingerie store nearby and was a patron. One fellow, a *Magnum P.I.* lookalike, corrected me when I rang up his drink at $4.60. "It should be five dollars even," he said. "I get the same drink every morning."

Many of our customers were young working people in their twenties and thirties. My coworker Aaron, who dressed in oversize black clothes and sported an untamed head of hair and an uncut goatee, called the neighborhood we were in "yuppie trash hell." *Yuppie* has become such a catchall word as to be almost not descriptive, but many of our customers were a subclass of young people who seemed to exult in the material trappings of upward mobility. They had good jobs, disposable income, and leisure time. The women took clothing cues directly from the pages of fashion magazines and television shows such as *Sex and the City*. That season, it was pajamalike outfits and oversized Jackie O. sunglasses. As for Aaron, he might have loathed our customers, but when he got promoted to the salaried position of an assistant manager at another store, he held court for a week. "I've been informing all of my regular customers that I am moving to the Polk Street store," he told me. "I just got married," he says. "I'm basically doing the career thing here for the money."

All through the store, people talked wildly into cell phones. Some gesticulated to invisible friends and colleagues, and many had to be politely interrupted midconversation for their order: "Oh my God! That is so not cool of him to do—" "Excuse me, can I help you?" We had a fair number of regulars, starting with the early-morning crew that showed up when our doors opened at 5:50.

They included a broad man with big hands who worked at the city's corporation yard and told me he had five Day-Glo orange shirts, one for each day of the week. There was a guy named Quinn who was mentally disabled. We helped him with quirky wishes such as filling his water bottle with filtered water and topping off his mint tea with soy milk. Our customers came to the store for a variety of reasons, some to work and some to socialize. For some it was for the communal feeling, where for four dollars they could plug into something bigger, a watering hole for urban nomads. Some were in and out after they bought a quick cup. Others stayed for hours, and some returned for sequential days, reading loose newspapers from our stack. Some came for a "third place," as Marty had explained that first day. The idea of a third place, I found after working there, was both compelling and distressing.

THIRD PLACES

According to sociologist Ray Oldenburg, third places are informal public gathering spots where people can feel at home. They are "core settings of informal public life." He has likened third places to the Greek agora and the Roman forum. In a book he wrote about the subject, he lamented the loss of many such places, such as taverns and teahouses, and the replacement with inferior substitutes. "Where once there were places, we now find *nonplaces*. In real places the human being is a person. . . . In *nonplaces*, individuality disappears." He wrote that if "there is no neutral ground in the neighborhoods where people live, association outside the home will be impoverished."

Starbucks chairman Howard Schultz was well aware of Oldenburg's writings as Starbucks blossomed from a small chain into the global force it is now. In his memoir, Schultz wrote, "Starbucks stores are not yet the ideal Third Place. We don't have a lot of seating, and customers don't often get to know people they meet there." By Oldenburg's definition, Starbucks stores are more nonplaces than third places. "The nonplace that takes over makes life a little less confusing, a little easier, for people new to the area," Oldenburg wrote. "A familiar logo beckons. It offers the predictable and the familiar to the nation's nomads, but it offers a real place to nobody." Nonplaces are expected to achieve maximum profits, he wrote, from transient customers, not a group of hangers-on. "What attracts the regular visitor to a third place is supplied not by management but by the fellow customers. The third place is just so much space unless the right people are there to make it come alive, and they are the regulars."

In 2006, Starbucks announced plans to eventually ramp up from its 12,000 stores in 37 countries to 40,000 stores worldwide. At the time of the announcement, the company said it recognized that its customer base "was broadening and becoming more diverse." Starbucks was seeing 40 million customers a week and employing more than 140,000 people. By 2006, coffee had become the second most actively traded commodity in the world, after oil. And according to the International Coffee Organization, since 1990, when Starbucks began its exponential growth, retail sales of coffee increased from $30 billion to $70 billion, and in 2006 some 1.6 billion cups of coffee were consumed a day, 400 million of those in the United States. And so the essential question vis-à-vis Starbucks is this: Can a third place be an isolated venue that also happens to be a part of a 12,000-store chain? What about a 40,000-store chain? Never in the history of the world has any single institution set about creating so many third places in such a concentrated, systematic push. If you have 140,000 employees and lease more than 10 million square feet of space, is it not an illusion to act small? Has Starbucks co-opted the idea of a third place without actually staying true to it?

For some, Starbucks is a third place, but for others it does not provide the needed sense of place to qualify. As a barista I heard one of my customers say, "I love where I live—I mean, hey, I can walk to Starbucks." Starbucks clearly played a positive role in his psychic universe. I heard others speak highly of "their" Starbucks cafés when visiting San Francisco. For some, a part of the equation seems disconnected when a corporation such as Starbucks artificially preserves a feeling of small town and community that does not really exist. In one posting on Craigslist, a barista seemed to cut the third place in two: "We are not your friends. We are usually not your neighbors. In most cases, we absolutely loathe you, but we are outwardly friendly—because we are paid to be." The corporate mission has been to get big and stay small, but is it false to try to maintain a level of intimacy with customers when you have a real goal of world domination? It was hard to work at Starbucks without feeling as if I was contributing to the urban and suburban homogenization so often blamed on the corporation.

Baristas bring the Starbucks experience to life for people who visit its stores. They put a human face on what might otherwise be viewed as a bland, monopolistic, globalizing corporation. By humanizing the customer experience, these "branded" employees allow the company to thrive. It's an interaction that can be put quite simply: When you buy a latte at Starbucks, your view of the company—its brand—is largely shaped by the person who serves you. You may have a vague sense of the founder's story, but by and large it's these front-line employees who connect you to the larger corporation. As part of my job as a barista, I was meant to "recognize new customers and take action to make them feel welcome." I could "exceed expectations" by "know[ing] customers by name or drink." At Starbucks, it is the employees who play a vital part in the third place concept, whether real or an illusion.

If you believe in Starbucks as a third place, it can be a great place to work. But if you feel that the customer service you are providing is fake, it's harder to be genuine. As for me, there were days when the customers made me want to run. Some days after taking yet another order for a silly, oversugared beverage, I looked at the long line of customers that seemed to never end, and I wanted to flee the store. As days turned into weeks at Starbucks, instead of bonding with my customers or even getting to know them, I felt more alienated. I began to loathe them as they treated themselves to the products we offered. The individualized orders and particulars so many customers seemed to cherish—having a coffee handmade just so—struck me as a societal illness underwritten by corporate greed. And the view from behind the counter, where we were more often than not rushing to slap together a drink instead of crafting it carefully, made me feel that the product was unworthy of what we charged. With so much focus on creating a welcoming place for our customers, I almost forgot we were a moneymaking operation. Despite the culture Starbucks works to create, the hidden aim of the stores is, of course, to vacuum dollars from the pockets of the customers into the black, electronically alarm-guarded safe in the back room, the true center of the stores—the real third place.

THE THIRD WAVE

Working at Starbucks and hearing so much about this idea of a third place, I was curious how the company chose its locations, how it decided what constituted an appropriate place to build a third place. If each Starbucks was a sort of coffee theater, I wondered who found the stages. After a bit of research I learned that in the Bay Area, one woman named Staci Eisler had chosen the locations for more than 300 of the 500 open Starbucks stores.

Several weeks into my time working at Starbucks, I arranged to head out with Eisler and, as a reporter, learn how she chose the locations. A small woman in her mid-thirties with a certain likeness to Shirley Temple, Eisler had a voice with a singsong pitch. She described to me how the behavior of suburban commuters adheres to patterns: Coffee shops should be on people's way to work, and oil changers and dry cleaners should be on the way home. As we drove, she took part in a speakerphone call with a real estate broker in a far-off city in California's Central Valley. He represented a shopping-mall owner and was doing everything possible to get Starbucks to set up shop in the mall. Unlike in the 1990s, she no longer scouts on behalf of an obscure company; now people clamor for a Starbucks to anchor their malls. The growth of strip malls and the homogenization of suburbs and cities that is often pinned on chains such as Starbucks happened like this—one conversation at a time.

Eisler and I drove through Mill Valley, a town 15 miles north of San Francisco. She pointed out how local opposition had kept the chain out of this town's downtown plaza but not several small shopping areas nearby. I asked her whether it was true that Starbucks waited for several other coffee shops to set up before moving into a given neighborhood, sending the other stores packing. She fumed; it was a sentiment she often heard but would not tolerate. Such thinking is not part of the equation, she said. Starbucks created a whole new segment of the marketplace and has launched more competitors than it has closed. Starbucks does not undercut prices—most of the time, its prices are higher. What is capitalism for anyway, she wanted to know, if not for competition? Any other way of looking at it would be socialism, not capitalism. "We are not the dog," she said cryptically, "but the tail wagging the dog."

Another way Starbucks finds locations is through acquisition, by buying smaller chains and gradually incorporating them. There was, in fact, a coffee shop just across the street and down several doors from where I worked named Torrefazione Italia. It served coffee in classic Italian ceramic cups and had outdoor tables and chairs that sprawled onto the sidewalk outside. Patrons there seemed a touch more relaxed than our customers; the shop was smaller and more intimate and felt like a place I would rather go than the Starbucks where I worked.

One day back in my store on Union Street, a woman came in, ordered a blueberry muffin, and presented her Starbucks employee ID card for a discount. I asked her where she worked, and she said across the street, at Torrefazione. "It's actually part of the company," she said. Though no signage linked the two, Starbucks had purchased the chain of 17 stores two years before.

Part of the initial purchase plan had been to keep the stores separate and to not draw any connection with Starbucks. But this was difficult for employees. One manager, Eileen Hassi, found herself listening often as customers told her how much they disliked Starbucks. She felt compelled to tell them that technically they were actually *in* a Starbucks. Starbucks corporate told all managers like her that they would not change anything, but changes slowly crept in. The dress code, which had been merely to look nice and use good judgment (collared shirts, no shorts) changed to all-black clothes and no denim. Soon enough, Starbucks policies had to be enforced—employees became partners, in the Starbucks lexicon, and new video cameras were installed that subtly changed the way employees and their customers behaved and related.

Hassi and other managers grew disillusioned, a feeling that was capped by attending the annual Starbucks managerial summit, a three-day meeting at Seattle's Key Arena, where the SuperSonics play. The three days were filled with speeches by executives, performances by Bob Dylan and Bruce Springsteen impersonators, and a motivational speech by activist Erin Brockovich. Hassi and her group of 17 from Torrefazione felt as if they were a small strain of a culture that had been improperly injected into a larger host that was attempting to attack it. The end was coming soon for Torrefazione Italia; within six months stores were either shut down or refashioned and its employees sent to work in the larger chain's green-hued retail outlets.

Hassi, who had worked at a café in Portland, Oregon, prior to Torrefazione, hatched a plan to open her own coffeehouse. She talked to Jeremy Tooker, another Torrefazione manager with a similar idea. To Hassi and Tooker, the sale and mass-marketing of coffee had moved through two waves and was entering a third. The first wave was the worldwide spread of the beverage and the eventual production of freeze-dried versions such as Sanka in the era after World War II. The second wave was the popularization and mass-marketing of higher-quality Arabica coffees and espresso beverages and café culture in the 1980s and 1990s that was chiefly Starbucks's doing. The third wave built on the groundwork that Starbucks laid; in this next wave, the quality of the coffee was paramount. In part the third wave was a response to the homogenization of the second wave. Its tenets include roasting beans on-site and paying close attention to roasted-on dates and site of origin. Hassi and Tooker were third-wavers, and they held strong feelings about how they might shape their own café. In May 2005 they opened Ritual Coffee Roasters in San Francisco's bohemian Mission District.

To understand Ritual's approach is to gain a bean's-eye view of the perfect cup of coffee. Critical differences start with the origin of the bean and the fair price negotiated with the grower and the way in which the coffee is roasted in small batches. This bean is more often than not grown among shady trees on a small plantation in a region such as the highlands of Guatemala. There, through what is known in the coffee business as direct trade, a coffee sourcer negotiates directly with a farmer to buy hundreds or even thousands of pounds of coffee. That coffee, once matured, is flown to the store, where the proprietors fire up a coffee-roasting machine and set the beans carefully inside to roast.

To make a double espresso, one of the baristas on staff at Ritual takes about a quarter cup of these beans and grinds them no more than 30 seconds before pouring them into a metal filter basket and then tamps the crushed beans. The basket is inserted in a La Marzocco espresso machine and a button is switched on that sends water, heated to 10 atmospheres of pressure, through the dry beans. The brown liquid that makes it through the gauntlet is coffee, in the form of a double espresso. It is best consumed within a minute; otherwise it will taste sour.

Knowing the Starbucks efficiency firsthand, as I had, I dropped by Ritual with an eye on how a system run by two former Starbucks employees might operate. The café, which opened in a former trendy furniture store, was decorated in a pre-end-of-the-USSR communist-chic décor: A hammer-and-sickle flag flew over the front door, and inside there was a lot of red and a dark wood counter that ran down the middle of the wide café. More than a year after it opened, Ritual had emerged as one of San Francisco's premier destination coffee shops.

I watched as workers scurried around attempting to keep up with the influx of trendy customers, young people in various modes of cool uniform, including vintage clothing and flattened, slept-on hair. Instead of a basic drip coffee, Ritual French-presses coffee in small amounts. Coffee is chiefly served in white china, necessitating one staff member who works the sink and dishwasher. As I watched I could see that coffee was running low—it had to be pressed and decanted into urns next to the cash register. The work-flow in the café seemed extremely slow. There was a line out the door, but the clientele were not put off by the wait. The place was doing strong business—the inefficient workflow did not seem too damaging, but I wondered how much more coffee could be sold with a smoother-flowing system like the one at Starbucks.

Hassi said she hired 17 employees in the first year Ritual was open and not one quit. With 100 percent retention, the workers were a bonded group that tended to spend nonworking hours to-gether. The employees were hired for their passion about coffee. "If they don't have any background in food service, that's okay," said Hassi. But if they are not passionate about coffee, that's another story. "When I ask them what they like about coffee and their eyes just kind of light up, those are the ones I hire."

Months later, I was in Seattle at the Pike Place Market, at what the company says is the first Starbucks store. This store had been built with a nautical theme to look as if it had been there for de-cades. And now, it has been there almost three decades. It's a small store with barely enough room for customers to queue up—no chairs, just a brass rail down the center.

Worldwide, there was just one Ritual, while there were 12,000 Starbucks coffeehouses. Ritual was a lens through which to view Starbucks's growth. Chairman Howard Schultz wrote that by 1995, "distracted by our size and ubiquity," customers "missed the point about our quality and commitment to community." What happens in 30 years if all coffee shops roast coffee on-site, if they are all third-wavers? Perhaps a fourth wave has already begun.

IN ADDITION TO the comprehensive employee manual that ex-plained how to make beverages, on my first day I was also given a slim book about the size of a passport. Its cover bore a close-up photograph of a worker's green apron with the embroidered Starbucks mermaid logo. Characteristic of the schism between wanting to be big and small at the same time was this artifact. "At first, you might think this is nonsense," Marty had said. "When I first saw it a few months ago, I thought it was pretty silly. 'I mean, what, do they think, that we are in kindergarten?' was what I was thinking. It's simple, but it's also a great little book. Check it out. Let me know what you think."

The book outlined five very specific points about our conduct as employees. The points were subtle but profound and spoke to the heart of the Starbucks mission: *Be welcoming. Be genuine. Be knowledgeable. Be considerate. Be involved.* The book instantly made me a bit more cynical about the working culture at Starbucks. But the *Green Apron Book* was more than just a corporate handout to inspire us: It was the basis for an employee reward system and a way of gauging employee participation in culture-building. It was a qualitative system to judge how well you met those five commands. If your supervisor recognized you for "being welcoming," you were one fifth of the way to receiving a special award pin. If you were recognized in all five areas, you received a Green Apron pin. Marty told me he had given the pin to only one employee in our store, Aaron, the shift supervisor.

One letter I happened to read, written by a regional manager, demonstrated the role of this book in store operations. In part, it read:

Dear Partners:

I love the Green Apron Book. *I love it because it is a reflection of our partners and the work you do each day to create the Starbucks experience and provide that human connection so needed in our world, one customer, one partner, one welcoming smile, and one cup of coffee at a time. . . . Speaking of the Green Apron, when you are*

*selecting new partners to the company, ensure [that] the people you
are inviting on board are a reflection of ALL that you and your
teams have created. AND, a reflection of how great you know it can
be. So, thanks for staffing your stores with the right people (people
that embody the principles laid out in the* Green Apron Book).

It was interesting to see such importance placed on this little
three-by-five-inch book. It shaped how people were hired, recognized, and promoted. While we were trying to be authentic and
welcoming, we were also meant to work hard and deliver hundreds
of steaming hot drinks each day. I came to wonder which was the
main Starbucks product—"authentic" employees or cups of coffee.
It was also clear from this note that some managers were hiring
people who were not, in fact, ideal workers. Some workers, I suspected, had come to the company just to work the 20 weekly hours
and gain health insurance, not because they believed in it.

The *Green Apron Book* is the kind of artifact indicative of a company in the process of rapidly manufacturing and maintaining a
culture. The book represents a clear distillation of those parts of the
current culture that the company hopes will be elevated and ampli-
fied. Being told to be authentic seems contradictory, especially in a
workplace that doesn't allow the exhibition of tattoos and body
piercing that many of the latest generation of workers have picked
up as means of self-expression. How can you be authentic and genuine if you have to wear a sweatband to cover the dragon tattoo
circling your wrist like my coworker Maurice did?

MIT professor Edgar Schein wrote that culture should be viewed
"as the accumulated shared learning of a given group, covering behavioral, emotional, and cognitive elements of the group members'
total psychological functioning. For shared learning to occur, there
must be a history of experience, which in turn implies some stability
of membership in the group." But with some exceptions, the front

lines are not a place for stable membership. Front-line employees share little history with one another and the company. It is an environment of constant turnover and constant training of new recruits, so the culture you experience on the front lines is best when it is shaped by the home office to be quickly injected into new recruits, either through immersion in orientation or on-the-job learning. The front lines are a subculture of the greater corporate culture.

Harvard professors James Heskett and John Cotter call culture the "common or pervasive ways of acting that are found in a group that persist because group members tend to behave in ways that teach these practices (as well as their shared values) to new members, rewarding those that fit in and sanctioning those that do not." But on the front lines there is not much time for this osmotic transfer of practices and values; the transfer has to be fast. For a front-line employee, culture is often just one's perception of the organization, a quick take that says this place is either for you or not.

In the best cultures, you believe without being persuaded to do so, but Starbucks seemed to work extra hard to ensure that we all would emerge as believers. If each culture at a corporation has an underlying model, an exemplary system from which it can draw, the Starbucks model may well be kindergarten. The kindergarten cultural archetype is about a place that would turn out softer, gentler, kinder employees. Representative of this kindergarten atmosphere were things such as the *Green Apron Book*. In our back room was a bulletin board that listed those lucky award recipients. But there seemed to be little objective means of evaluating us for these awards. In practice, it was a small circle of five or six employees who seemed to receive and nominate one another, and the bulletin board gave testimony to this:

Monique, thanks for being so involved in all the contests we've had.

—Erika

Elizabeth, thank you for making the best foam on earth.

—Marty

Amy, thanks for being so welcoming to our new partners.

—Marty

Erika, thanks for always being so considerate!

—Monique

MY COFFEE MASTER

Though my training was no more robust, soon enough I had moved from working afternoons to chiefly mornings. Start times were at 5 and 6:30 AM and—least ideally—at 4:15 to open for the day. When we met at 4:15, there was no time for hanging out or even having a cup of coffee. Two or three of us met in front of the locked store. Once we opened the door and turned off the alarm, we were immediately on task. Overnight deliveries had arrived, including stacks of milk crates and a towering eight-foot stack of baked goods in plastic flats that all needed to be sorted out and put on plates in our pastry case: Asiago bagels, oatmeal cookies, blueberry muffins, peach galettes.

When I was regularly clocking in before sunrise, the excitement of my undercover job had faded: At 4:15 AM, I definitely worked there. By 5:50 we were open for business, and I was working the register, butterflies building into some form of retail stage fright as I anticipated the commuter crowd. I plowed through our morning rush with a fair amount of finesse. I was getting faster at writing out the drink orders on the paper cups and at punching orders into the register. At 9 AM Marty asked me if I wanted a break from the register, to work downstairs in the basement. "Don't get discouraged. You won't always have to work on register," he said. "You are doing a great job," he said. His compliment, as small as it was, was a tonic to my tired body and mind. Strangely, though everything I learned was new and I was constantly performing in front of a live audience, I had received little feedback.

Erika was the reason our store worked as well as it did. At 29 she was a short, pear-shaped woman who wore her long, wavy, dyed-blond curls at shoulder length or pulled tightly back into a ponytail with bangs. She had wide blue eyes and applied dark mascara to her lashes. Technically speaking, Erika was our assistant manager; but her role overshadowed that of Marty, our more distant manager, who ruled, as far as I could tell, by fear. Erika was Marty's lieutenant, but I came to see her more as a den mother, there to shepherd our wayward troupe along the Starbucks way. Erika was a living, breathing embodiment of all that Starbucks was about. She hewed to a higher authority than our manager. As I worked with her, I tried to understand her level of devotion.

Though our store might be physically removed from the other branches of the corporate tree, people like Erika tied us right in. She was always there to answer my questions and to show me how to do things, to correct me if I deviated from the prescribed rules of the organization, and to bring me deeper into the fold. At various times she told me to tuck in my shirt, not to wear a dirty apron, and not to let customers see me drinking coffee. In my notes, I wrote, "Erika is a hard-ass, but she is the heart and soul of training" and "Erika: without her we'd be screwed."

One day a couple of weeks into my time at Starbucks, I came into the store and saw Erika wearing a black apron, not the traditional green that the rest of us wore. After months of study and a daylong final exam, Erika had been awarded the prized black apron of the "Coffee Master." Arriving back from testing, Erika was more fired up than I had ever seen her. Her face glowed with a new sense of purpose that came with on-the-job accomplishment.

She also seemed bent on pushing us into more advanced on-the-job learning. Her new level pushed her to push us more.

"Alex, what have you tasted this week?" Erika asked between the rhythmic pulses of customers. "We all need to be tasting coffee, and tasting it every shift. We need to fill out a coffee passport every 90 days."

The coffee passport was another small booklet in which we were meant to take down notes and observations about the coffee we sampled on the job. It told us that it was a guide to our "coffee learning journey" and a place to put down notes on the "wonderful beverage in all its forms." The book listed 25 coffees and left room for seasonal and new offerings.

When Erika ran a shift, we were encouraged to dig into a drawer of coffee bags or open a fresh bag and brew a French press of coffee to taste. Erika took the initiative and pressed an eight-cup metal cylinder of coffee. After the prescribed eight minutes, she decanted the steaming brown fluid into double-walled Dixie cups for those of us working. Coffee tastings unfolded formally or casually. Sometimes a group of us circled up, each clutching a cup filled with fresh coffee. The proper way to taste, we were taught, involved three steps: First you were to cup the steaming coffee under your nose and with your palm deflect the vapor into your nostrils while you took a strong whiff and registered the aroma. Second, you took the cup to your lips and sucked and slurped in the liquid and sprayed the liquid all over your palate. Third, you drank the coffee.

My own notes were limited by my undeveloped palate. My coffee passport had the most basic of entries, largely parroted terms that I heard my superiors tossing around or that I read on the back of labels. I had little real sense of these things myself: *"Smells sweet. Hint of blackberry. Nutty—like Guatemala. Tastes smoky? Telltale African fruitiness and acidity. Earthy/dirty/almost burned. Lemon comes out with lemon scone. Little chunks of dirt. North Tanzania = volcanic soil."*

It was hard not to feel a bit humbled in the face of all this arcane coffee knowledge. I was suddenly given to the grand ambition of one day being able to blind-identify coffee—to study at the feet of a guy like Ed Faubert, a coffee buyer I read about in a news article who works for the New York Board of Trade. People like him speak in terms of cleans, dirtiness, flats, mustiness, brightness, and acidity and can determine blindly not only that a particular spoonful of coffee came from Guatemala but also that it came from the Atitlán region, at the altitude of 4,500 feet, and was grown on a north-facing slope. Eventually, I suppose, had I applied myself harder and stayed at Starbucks longer, my tasting notes would have coalesced into more profound knowledge. Though largely a culture built on a kindergarten-like rewards system, the knowledge we could accrue at Starbucks was not so basic. I would have been able, at least, to tell customers knowingly about the "radical smoothness of the mild roast that comes out of Kenya's Rift Valley." But the realities of day-to-day work and long task-filled shifts precluded study. Beyond broad differences in coffee blends, after six weeks, I was still pretty much stumped.

IN AN IDEAL world, all new Starbucks employees begin an apprenticeship of sorts when they join the company, learning how to make the different coffee and tea drinks. All Starbuckses now use automatic espresso machines that grind coffee and produce shots on demand, so the barista no longer needs to tamp and grind each shot of espresso. But there is still a lot to learn because there are hundreds of requests and specific ways to execute them.

I spent almost all of my time on the register, and even after a month I had worked at the bar only a little. Erika told me I had to ask to be on the bar, but it was hard to work at the bar because I didn't know what I was doing. Being a barista means multitasking, and it's hard to multitask when you barely know the tasks. I learned in fits and starts. My coworker Nora was my chief tutor when it came to learning how to make espresso drinks. Informal training started with me standing alongside her at the bar and decoding the cups that came to her. Then I started to prepare those drinks I could easily execute. By the time I was with Nora, I had studied the drink menu and memorized drinks and notations for them, which we translated from customers' verbal requests into Starbucks shorthand. (A % sign, for example, denoted low-fat milk if a customer didn't want the default 2% milk we served.) Nora was from Vancouver, where she was midway through college at the University of British Columbia and often compared how they did things in her Vancouver store to how we did things in San Francisco. She was a very mature woman for 22 and seemed to have an eye on being promoted to shift supervisor. I had a long way to go in learning all the drinks and people's special orders and their requests for extra hot, extra foam, and extra care. Nora was a good teacher, but I kept floundering trying to remember if the Americano's default was three shots and whether I needed to add ice before or after I pulled the shot for an iced mocha. In a job that lacked intellectual stimulation, such as this one at Starbucks, the pleasure for me came from mastering and perfecting a craft and by being able to use that craft to create quality products. But hurdles to learning stood in the way. I am one who enjoys tending bar at parties, and at Starbucks there were a few times when I felt joy in my own craftsmanship, but such moments were fleeting.

After making drinks all afternoon with Nora one day, I asked her if I could crank out a double cappuccino for myself right before break. She very seriously explained that I could not and reminded me that I had to go around to the other side of the register to place my order. "We'll never get to know the customer's perspective if we don't order it from that side, you know?" she said. This policy meant that sometimes you had to get in line and wait for half of your 15-minute break to order a drink. But it was interesting: When I ordered from a few of my female colleagues, they presented a completely different face, a sort of come-hither, how-may-I-help-you look. And when I waited on my superiors, such as Marty and Erika, I felt nervous and suspected that they were grading me, testing me, and timing me. Just about everyone working in the store had a drink they called their own. More than a few coworkers asked me what mine was, and I felt the need to choose something more exotic than a double espresso.

Some of my colleagues performed with finesse at the bar, but I was far from there. One afternoon after we had worked a few hours together, I sat with a newly transferred shift supervisor named Maurice. He had been cranking at the bar for hours, his hands moving left and right and forward and back toward the espresso machines like a prizefighter pressed up against an opponent at the end of a match.

"Man," I said, "you were getting schooled out there."

"That was nothing," he replied. "That was fun."

I didn't have the skills yet, and I was envious of Maurice and how he could get into a work flow that eluded me.

In my first week on the job I had gone to something called "The Starbucks Experience Workshop," a regional orientation lasting half a Saturday. Though I hoped it would be a day of skill-building, it was more a day of culture-building. Training started at 8 AM.

In the elevator up, I met Zac and Rob. Like me, they were late. They commiserated about a big night of drinking as Zac pulled out a pair of black dress shoes for Rob that he had borrowed from his roommate, a culinary student.

The last to file into the classroom, we sat around a horseshoe-shaped table and joined other new hires watching the end of a DVD showing Starbucks employees around the world. *"Guten tag,"*

they said, *"Konichiwa," "Buenas dias!"* Our instructor was a Latina
in her early forties who spoke with a hard-to-listen-to accent that
sounded like Kermit the Frog. She pointed to the video monitor
and said, "Hopefully you are seeing a third place being created in
each store."

We had all followed the dress code: a white or black collared shirt
and black or khaki pants. Most everyone was 18 to 22 years old,
except for me and two women in their early forties who had met
working out at Curves. We all said our names, named the store
where we would be working, and named a person with whom we
would like to enjoy a hypothetical cup of coffee. There was a guy
named Justin with long bleached-blond hair; a chubby, thick guy
named Josh who never opened his mouth all morning; a film student
named Kirsten; and Jessica, a woman with curly brown hair who had
just moved from Oregon. One guy said he would share a cup with
his dad, another said his best friend, and the art student said movie
director Tim Burton. Zac and Rob sat on my left. Zac was also a film
student at a local art school, and Rob attended San Francisco State.
They had met the week before, during training at their new state-of-
the-art Starbucks store, and were fast friends.

We watched DVDs that detailed the many facets of Starbucks,
and our instructor pulled out lessons to share. One DVD showed
where beans were grown on a Guatemalan farm. "People have
asked me," our instructor said, "whether I have gone to other countries to see how Starbucks treats the farmers who grow our coffee. I
have not been there, but I think if there was any problem, journal-
ists would find out about it, like they did at Nike with the sweat-
shops." Our instructor used the first-person collective, *we*. But we,
the new employees, were still outsiders. To us the company remained "they."

We sampled coffee as a group and compared Starbucks Light-
Note Blend to what our instructor called "typical commercial

coffee"—watered-down pond water that was easy to differentiate because it tasted like cardboard. We split into teams of three and practiced brewing coffee in French presses set up in the classroom.

Zac and Rob seemed like the kind of guys who would prefer to work at an independent coffee shop, but they were excited to start at Starbucks. "Dude, at our new store, we are trying out these new aprons," Zac told me. "They've got pockets." But both were aware that the facts we were being taught were a form of propaganda. At one point Rob's task was to study some documents and explain to the group the differences between two coffees. "House Blend is a medium-bodied blend of Latin American coffees with a round smoothness; Verona is a Latin American and Asia Pacific blend of coffees with a touch of Italian Roast for added depth," he reported.

After he sat down, Zac turned to Rob: "Damn, man, you really sounded like you knew what you were talking about. Either you really know your shit or you are a good actor!"

"Well," Rob said, "I guess I'm a good actor. I had no idea what I was talking about."

"You totally convinced me!" said Zac.

The duo had stumbled on the barista-as-actor notion: *We might not know much, but if we can act the part in this coffee theater, we'll do just fine.* "People just say 'earthy' because it's a nicer way of saying 'dirty,'" said Rob.

The content of the class made it clear that one of Starbucks' goals for the day was to undercut criticism of the company; the DVDs acted as a hedge against employees' believing any blasphemous remarks they might have heard elsewhere. The DVDs emphasized the company's many charitable activities and employee benefits. Our instructor told us that Starbucks was better than mom-and-pop companies because at Starbucks you could move around; we would have career growth opportunities and other benefits we would never get from smaller companies. When she worked at a family restaurant and it closed, she said, she had nothing to show for her time there. Now she managed a store in San Francisco. She said that she couldn't be promoted unless she promoted her staff.

Finally our instructor prepared to send us out, back to our stores. "Just have fun," she told us. "And when you go to work, just act as if you are throwing a big party for all of your friends and they are coming over to enjoy a cup of coffee with you!" To this last over-the-top command, Zac added, in a blazing act of insubordination: "And don't forget to charge them a shitload of money!"

WE WORK IN A SUBMARINE

One especially hot day when I arrived at 9 AM, I could tell that we were under fire, yet the team was holding tight. I cut through the lines outside and the people bunched at the end of our counter, expectant, waiting for drinks to come off the end of our liquid assembly line. I waved hello to Miles, Gonzalez, and Celia, who were all working hard. My first duty was to clock in and then take a drawer, or till, from the register, and count it in back using an incredibly precise scale that could sense the weight of a single dollar bill. Miles was the shift supervisor. He was also working as our expediter, and he was handling it like a pro, taking orders and writing them on the cups and passing those to Gonzalez at the bar, while also filling white bags with baked goods. Once I was on the floor and on the register, all I would have to do was ring people up as fast as I could. At peak, we moved through 150 customers an hour and upward of 1,000 transactions per day.

Our music system had been upgraded, and a ska mix, one of the few mixes I actually enjoyed, was in rotation. It was the English Beat, then Bob Marley, Lee "Scratch" Perry belting out "Police and

Thieves," and the Specials singing an apt version of "Rat Race": "Working for the rat race/You know you're wasting your time."

"Help me look good," said Miles. "I only started last week." He had moved from St. Louis and was being tested as a shift supervisor by our in-store leaders. I had every intention of helping him look good. It was a blistering hot day out, one of the few we saw in San Francisco, and people were coming in droves to hydrate on our sugary beverages.

On this day of much heat and many liquids, I flowed with the work. I could feel my actions leading to tips. I was flirting and being funny and providing excellent service by asking if people wanted room for cream and all the other stuff I had not been able to do in the past in my rush to just get the drinks out. I was selling $1.40 bottles of water that were not cold because we were selling so many that we could not chill them all, and I was asking whether people would "like a glass of ice with that," and many seemed quite pleased by this extra service. As the day went on I moved cautiously to the bar myself, and Miles kept an eye on me as I made a string of lattes and cappuccinos. I waited for the complaints to mount— "Hey, this cappuccino is too wet"—but they failed to materialize. I was getting better at it.

Operating at full throttle, we were like a submarine crew plunging steadfastly under icy Arctic waters as torpedoes whizzed past our sleek craft. We were primed and ready. Through the Starbucks model we had married warmth with speed and efficiency, and for the most part it worked well.

There was no doubt that we were stealing customers from less-efficient operations, such as the café around the corner that was open for half the number of hours we were, and where customers waited in line idly for five minutes before talking to a server. Not at our store. At Starbucks there were tasks to attend to at every minute

and every second, and work-flow studies had allowed the corporation to break these tasks down into incremental steps. Everything
was systematized and codified, and there were rules and processes
and feedback loops.

We plowed through gallons of milk and had to haul out both ice
and milk regularly from the back room to the front. We had a
number of small timers that we clipped onto coffee urns so that
they would alert us to rebrew every hour. We poured unused coffee
down the drain. Every 10 minutes another buzzer went off (usually
clipped to the shift supervisor's apron), and one of us was dispatched
into the café to wipe down tables, check (and clean) the restrooms,
restock the refrigerated cases, resupply packets of sugar, check milk
thermos levels, and organize our condiment bar. There were precise orbits, and like planets in a perfect Starbucks solar system, we
spun elliptically and never made contact.

Midway through this shift, Miles handed me a list of items
needed from our supply room: 3 venti cups, 3 grande flat lids, 1 vanilla, 1 peppermint, 2 white mocha, 3 lemonade, 1 box honey, pastry
bags, 4 tall lids (hot), 1 hazelnut, 2 mocha mix. I made my way
through the back of the store and then downstairs to the vast, dimly
lit basement given over to metal shelves stocked with coffee cups,
piles of cardboard to be recycled, lockers we could use on our break,
and a table and chairs.

Nora was in back counting our crew's tips for the week. We had
a square plastic tip jar in front of our cash register, and many of our
customers tipped us. Some did it consciously, others reflexively
dumped in the change we gave them. Each day the tips were
bagged in special translucent Starbucks tip bags and put into the
safe. Though most restaurants divvy up tips in a manner that con-
nects them directly to the servers associated with specific customers,
at Starbucks tips are pooled and divided into employee hours
worked. Once a week the bags of change had to be counted, and it

was Starbucks's policy to pay one employee for the time it took to hand-count these tips. Nora's hands were black with dirt from handling coins. After Nora had concluded her count and done the necessary division, coworkers wanted to know the hourly tip amount for each of us, a rate that varied with how many worker-hours had been worked, how well the group had performed, and how many customers had come in. When I first started, I was told that tip averages were $2.50 per hour, but it was usually about $2.10. For me, that meant one fifth of my take-home pay was supplied by our customers.

When I was downstairs I could hear the shuffling and motion of the place on the hardwood floors above. It was strange to step out midshift, to be "off the floor." I felt like an actor who had left the stage or a soccer player gone to the locker room while the team played on. Downstairs was the rare place in the store where you were working but not directly tied to other partners.

There were laminated charts hung in our back room called deployment maps. They looked like hockey play-by-play diagrams and were covered with small, blocky circles and arrows. They outlined where partners should be, depending on staffing levels, and when we should use a floater, a position also called an expediter that stood at the heart of the Starbucks workforce efficiency system. The expediter had to be the most skilled partner, the multitasker among multitaskers. There wasn't a whole lot left to chance.

We were not always so good. I was the third partner to arrive one morning and I showed up at 6 AM; Susan and Armando had been there since 4:15. It was the Saturday of Independence Day weekend, and our manager, Marty, had made the questionable decision to leave town, bringing in a replacement. Fernando, his stand-in shift supervisor, came from another store (technically a "borrowed partner") and either did not care about the Starbucks standards I had learned or did not know them very well. Possibly because he was not in

his native store, Fernando was flailing. By 8 AM our system was se-
verely taxed. A longer line than I had yet seen snaked out the front
door. Typically Saturday mornings were slower than weekdays, but
on this holiday weekend every visiting tourist to San Francisco had
chosen our store as the beachhead for his or her own trip to the City
by the Bay.

Once one of our systems failed, it could quickly lead to another
failure; if we were out of cups and had to hustle downstairs to get
them, our line grew, we neglected to fill our milk thermoses, customers complained about this, we left the register to get milk, and
the line kept growing. By 9 AM, the three of us were struggling with
the most basic of things—cup supplies were dwindling, coffee urns
were running low, and none of us had taken a break. Fernando, for
his part, seemed content to hide behind the towering espresso machines. Instead of managing our descent into chaos, he staffed the
espresso bar while engaged in a Sisyphean effort to put an end to
the long line of white paper cups that ran from my station at the
cash register.

Not only were our physical systems starting to buckle under
pressure but also our mental and spiritual core was being chal-
lenged. It was a simple matter of having the wrong number of
staff members on hand, and our ship was heading swiftly down.
As this occurred, each of us silently placed the blame on the
others. I directed my frustration toward Fernando because he
seemed unable to take control of the situation and was unaware
that I was a new partner in need of more supervision. Susan directed her ire at Fernando for supervising poorly, our absent
manager for creating the situation, and me because I was still
learning and unable to move at the required speed. "It was
hard—I mean, we had a borrowed partner and a new partner,"
Susan said later. We moved rapidly from being in command of

the situation to having the situation command us. Though I might have enjoyed stepping back and appreciating the morning for what it was—an understaffed Starbucks store under siege by holiday customers—I was at that point so intimately part of the store that it would have been difficult to separate myself from the unfolding chaos. It was also hard to separate yourself when customers were directing their anger and impatience at you.

TO THE AVERAGE customer, things were probably looking fine, if busy, in the store. But I had just been shown the most recent "Customer Snapshot," a quarterly review of the store conducted anonymously and secretly by a visiting patroller. As our lines grew and the café's cleanliness fell away, I thought to myself: *What if a guy comes in right now to do a snapshot audit? We'd get creamed.* To the trained employee, such as I was becoming, things were getting worse by the minute.

The Snapshot is a systematic catalogue of the store and its ability to please the customer. There are four objective categories noted in a Snapshot: service, product quality, cleanliness, and speed of service. A fifth subjective category rates the store, awarding one to five stars for its presentation of "legendary service." As the printed Snapshot notes: "Customer Snapshot is a performance measure designed to evaluate the service experience we deliver to customers . . . [and] supports our BHAG and Mission Statement by measuring those items that create enthusiastically satisfied customers."

BHAG (big hairy audacious goal) was a term created and popularized by business guru Jim Collins to mean a goal worth betting the company on:

Like climbing a big mountain or going to the moon, a BHAG may be daunting, and perhaps risky, but the adventure, excitement, and challenge of it grabs people in the gut, gets their juices flowing, and creates immense forward momentum. Visionary companies have judiciously used BHAGs to stimulate progress and blast past the comparison companies at crucial points in history.

Though it's not written down, Starbucks's BHAG is about building an enduring emotional connection with customers.

Feeding into the Snapshot score are things such as whether the register partner and barista verbally greet you, make eye contact, thank you, are neat and clean, and display knowledge of products. To evaluate the product quality, the visitor measures whether the drink temperature falls into a designated zone of 135 to 170 degrees Fahrenheit (for most drinks) and whether the drink weighs in at an appropriate range within 50 grams (a tall decaf mocha, for example, is supposed to weigh between 334 and 384 grams). Each Starbucks store is essentially a remote factory, and the Snapshot taker is the roving quality-control inspector.

The visitor also evaluates the cleanliness of the store and the speed of service. Customers are supposed to wait a maximum of three minutes from the time they step into line to the time they receive their drink from the barista. In the most recent Snapshot, taken at 10:13 one Wednesday morning, Nora had been the partner evaluated, our manager told me, and she had done all the right things. The Snapshot included comments such as "the barista initiated conversation with customers by asking how their day was going," "the floor was free of debris," and "the back service counter was organized." Most customers didn't know that we had to wipe down the condiment bars every 10 minutes, and the fact that customers have probably been to dozens of other Starbucks in the course of their lives and generally had positive experiences buoyed us. Feedback loops like Starbucks's Snapshots are crucial when your way of judging employee productivity is gauged not only in sales and dollars but also in happy customers.

THOUGH IT'S SURELY different at other stores, at the store where I worked there was no real sense of camaraderie, one that, before I joined, I had assumed pervaded Starbucks and made it a great workplace. Perhaps the lack of camaraderie was caused by our high turnover. In just the couple of months that I was at Starbucks, about half of the 20 partners on staff left. Faces and names changed: Out went Nina, then Aaron (to assistant-manage the nearby store), then Whitney (back home to Seattle to work at another store), then Lucy (to Boston, where she was to keep working at a Starbucks while in graduate school). And in came Doug, Maurice, Chris, Dan, and Miles. Tim and Paul were brand new to the company. When I came in and saw them both sitting in khakis and white button-down shirts studiously focused on their training manuals it made me think that we were all participants in a vast retail experiment run by a core group in the Seattle headquarters, an experiment in which our training and performance was all quantifiable and visible to people we would never meet. To them I was simply "Partner 1274501."

Within a couple of days of Tim's arrival, I found myself training him and showing him how to count the money in the till and re-stock essential items such as coffee lids. As I did so, I recognized that I was, for the first time, training someone else and passing on what I had learned. I made an effort to be more friendly to him than the people who had been training me had been. Some of my coworkers had taken the time to show me the right way to do things and even point out shortcuts, while others had surprised me by being less than forthcoming with important details. One particular woman, Suzette, seemed to take pleasure in bossing me around and telling me, on a couple of occasions, that I was clueless. As I trained Tim I also realized that I was no longer the glaringly new guy, that whether I was ready for it or not, I was moving up in the ranks.

To attract new applicants, our manager put a sticker on our front window that said "Dream Venti." (Venti is the word Starbucks trademarked for its largest, 20-ounce drinks.) I doubted this slogan referred to the anxiety-filled dreams I had come to have often. Starbucks infiltrated my subconscious, and memorable, nightly sleep-altering dreams became stress filled and work related. Certainly, starting work at predawn hours and having easy access to strong coffee were not the perfect way to cope as I rode the learning curve. Often dreams involved oversleeping on those nights when I had to wake up at 3:30 in the morning. On the first night of a climbing trip with three friends, camped at 11,000 feet, I tossed and turned all night, plagued by Starbucks dreams. I went in and out of awareness, thinking that my tent-mate Scott was a customer. First he wanted a Frappuccino, then a cappuccino, a latte, a house drip, a pound of Sumatra beans ground for a Mr. Coffee. Confused and tired, at 4 AM I finally got to sleep.

As an outsider I was under the impression that people who worked at Starbucks would be made out of plastic or somehow automatons. I'd never been a loyal Starbucks customer, but I'd purchased cups of coffee at more than 50 of its stores all over the country, and the similarities of the many brief experiences led me to believe that a certain lack of individuality united the vast corps of Starbucks employees. The store environments are so similar that I assumed they would be necessarily stocked with a crew of act-alike drones. Going in to work at Starbucks, I couldn't shake that preconception. Even as I got to know my coworkers, I treated them warily. Surely they must be plastic, I thought—otherwise why would they work for this massive company? But I could hardly find a plastic member of our crew. Even after I left, I had to go back and review my notes to really believe it: Miles, Maurice, Gonzalez, Erika, Nora—each was very much an individual. But our manager was another story.

Marty, in expediter mode, jumped around like a hyper, robotic, overtrained monkey. When Marty worked behind the counter, you had the sense that he was adjusting his behavior to maximize Snapshot results, performing in such a way that if one of those quarterly undercover Snapshot takers came into our store when he was in the critical welcoming position, he would receive strong marks. He would be documented: "Caucasian male, height 5' 9" to 6'." Notes would read: "The barista asked me how my weekend was. The barista said, 'What can I get for you?'" But Marty, as effective as he might have been in this role, was far from genuine. To stand next to him was to hear a replay of and variations of the same string of messages as you'd expect from a robot: "Hello. How was your weekend? How's it going there? Good morning!" Absent was real care beneath this constant patter. Marty was an employee bent on hitting the numbers, but he had himself failed to heed the message: "Be authentic."

As for me, I too was far from authentic. Hired under somewhat false pretenses, I never could be myself in front of coworkers or customers. The store environment was one in which I'd never blossom into anything resembling an authentic version of myself. No matter how long I stayed on, it was unlikely I would shed my cynicism toward the heavy-handed culture-building that governed our performance as employees. I knew that one day long ago, Starbucks had been a truly authentic, interesting, and one-of-a-kind café, but that authenticity had been imitated and copied to a point where it was sadly lost and replaced with a new faux authenticity. So at the end of one Sunday-morning shift, I rolled up my two green aprons and inserted them into a manila envelope, jotted down a brief good-bye note to Marty and Erika on a Post-it, and did my part to boost the monthly turnover rate before going off in search of my true, authentic self.

SIX

IN THE RED ZONE

"I don't know how he does it," my coworker Shane said as we stared at the weekly sales figures, a long roster of the 40 of us who worked in the Apple Store and tabulations of how much cash each of us had brought in. In front of Shane's name, and in front of my name, there was a long line of zeroes. But next to another guy's name there was a stream of digits and dollar signs. One of our managers had taken a highlighter pen, covered this guy's name in pink, and drawn an arrow to where he had written, "Go, Naked Man!"

Naked Man's name was Leon, and in the past week he had sold several computers and all sorts of added-on warranties and extra "attachments." He had even sold these add-ons "naked"—that is, to people who did not buy a computer. Shane and I were in the back room, the employees-only "back of house" where we signed in for work and retrieved inventory. Shane had been there only a few weeks and I was in my first week. As part of more than a week of training, I would spend the next couple of hours shadowing Leon, so I would get a chance to see the Naked Man in action, to see just how he did it.

Leon walked in and, like me, was wearing a black Apple-issued T-shirt with a subtle white logo. The T-shirt was about all we had in the way of a uniform or a dress code, but it was enough to set us apart from customers. I hadn't really felt a part of the store until I put on a T-shirt three days into my employment. With a T-shirt you were indigenous; without one you were an outsider. Leon was about six feet tall and a wide, pillowy man with a cartoonlike, animated appearance. His head perched on top of his slim neck, he wore his hair short but spiked up a good half inch, and his lips seemed to peel away from each other. "Are you ready to go? Then let's do it!" He swung the door open onto the sales floor, and bounced foot to foot. If there was anything about him that screamed *salesman*, I could not see it. But his name was right next to our back room door, etched in brass on a wood plaque—Leon had been lead seller last month.

After the stint at Starbucks, I'd hoped to land at a workplace that had a strong culture but did not expend so much effort in building what amounted to a fake sense of belonging. The Apple Store was an obvious last stop in my expedition into the workplace. In the times I'd set foot in an Apple Store, even to just check my email while on the road, I'd had the feeling that the workers were at ease, even enchanted to be taking part in what seemed to be more of a cultural happening than the retail success story that it was rapidly becoming.

Apple first rolled out retail stores in 2001; five years later, it had grown into a chain of more than 175 high-grossing stores. The Apple retail store addressed what customers wanted in an ideal computer store experience. It was an Internet café of sorts, a computer seller, and a one-stop I.T. department. The store's layout was novel and easily perceived by any visitor; this was a store in which to hang out and to relax amid Apple products. Filled with just glass, wood, and stainless steel, it was a small-, not big-box, store. Apple recognized that modern customers no longer read manuals and wanted to be shown how to do things. I had been a customer and had sensed that workers were either cut from a different cloth or trained in a new way. Going to an Apple Store felt like dropping into the computer science department of a university; as much information was being shared as products were being sold. In the Apple equation, store workers were in-person teachers who, after working with customers, could foster strong consumer loyalty to the brand. The attitude of store employees had been as well thought out as the iPod user interface: Workers didn't seem to be working or selling, just hanging out and dispensing advice.

The store had a distinct metallic aroma, like a fragrance distilled from the inside of a cardboard computer box. The store was packed with people. Leon and I walked across the store and entered the so-called red zone, the area closest to the front door. Here in the red zone we were meant to keep our focus toward the door at all times with the hope of greeting any incoming faces, deterring any shoplifting attempts, and steering any interested customers toward sales. Shadowing Leon was just part of an exhaustive training program. He told me he had been with the store for just over four months. Soon enough we had a live customer standing in front of us.

"Welcome to the Apple Store," said Leon.

"Hello. I want to buy a computer. I've been waiting for a while, and I finally got the check," this customer said. She was a 55-year old woman wearing a loose white blouse, and, librarian-like, she had a pair of reading glasses on a slender cord around her neck. "Okay!" said Leon.

"So I can find out what kind of a computer is best for you, would it be all right if I ask you what you will be using your new computer for?" The customer told us that she ran a business out of her home and that her current PowerBook had stopped working. Leon was approaching the customer just as I had seen done in the training videos: He set up his position by explaining why he was asking so many questions, got the customer's permission, and then probed. "Do you need to have a computer that is portable?" he asked. "Do you do graphics or video work?" *Position, permission, probe.*

In the next 20 minutes Leon and I learned all sorts of things about our customer. Some of it was unearthed through Leon's probing, but most was simply volunteered by the customer. Some of it was germane to a sale, some not. We learned that she was an executive coach and had been educated at and now taught at a life-coaching institution in Santa Barbara. By the end of our sale, Leon leveraged this information to convince her to buy all the attachments that we offered: an extended warranty, an email and online storage account, and a service that would allow her to sign up for private lessons to learn about her computer. He even offered her an educator's discount. At the end of a half hour, our customer had spent more than $3,000, thanked Leon for his time and help, and then walked out of the store smiling. For his part, Leon sold what our manager termed a "rockslide"—not only a CPU (central processing unit) but also all three attachments. Leon printed out a copy of the receipt and hung it like a trophy in the manager's office. Go, Naked Man!

Reading material and videos in training provided plenty of background on how to sell, but it still looked difficult to master. Leon made it look easy. Sure, he spoke confidently, never mumbled, had deep knowledge of Apple products, and was able to answer any question a customer threw at him. He was also a person to whom other people came for answers; he was a beacon of the sales floor. All of that was true. But it was also true that a customer happened to walk in and say she wanted to buy a computer. People *come* to Apple stores to buy computers. How hard could it be? Why did Leon dominate though others did not?

BACK OF HOUSE

As a part-time Mac specialist, my responsibilities included providing "complete and appropriate solutions for every customer," translating "techno-speak into laymen's terms," and the "ability to teach and demonstrate to all levels of experience." Getting a job at one of the Apple Stores was not as difficult as I imagined it would be; It just took some persistence. I applied several times online by answering a few basic questions, pasting in a résumé, and selecting both the jobs and locations to which I wanted to apply. I eventually got a call. Stonestown Apple Store, in an upscale San Francisco mall, was ramping up for back-to-school and needed to hire three Mac specialists. I had two interviews with the store's assistant managers and was soon offered a job.

The store had a variety of workers. As a Mac specialist, I was the bottom-level computer salesperson. Moving up in terms of knowledge and responsibilities were those employees who taught in-store classes; the stock-room and inventory people; "creatives," who taught one-on-one lessons on how to use the computers and other Apple devices; "geniuses," responsible for diagnosing and fixing hardware and software problems; people in charge of store visuals; business salespeople who worked with small businesses; the training team who trained us; and two levels of store manager. Our manager was a short, skinny woman in her mid-thirties who had a blond bob; wore tight jeans, large belt buckles, and high-fashion eyeglasses; and looked most like a contemporary Raggedy Ann doll. We had three assistant managers as well: John-Luke had the wild hair of a mad scientist; Philip was a smooth dresser; and Frank was an extroverted dude with a soul patch.

Hiring workers had been easy for Apple—the company claimed to turn away 90 percent of applicants. The company was not looking for great salespeople using sophisticated technology, as one would imagines it easily could; instead it isolates true enthusiasts and true believers in Apple products, of which there are many. Whereas a place like Starbucks or Home Depot may have a harder time finding believers, Apple finds them easily and then builds them into salespeople from the ground up. Here, unlike Gap, CEO Steve Jobs could not slip in unannounced—he was revered as godlike. As workers, all we had to bring to the table was a passion for Apple products; the company supplied the knowledge we needed to teach, share, and sell to customers. By the time they were done training us we were computer salespeople, but you would hardly know it from how we acted. If Leon didn't seem like a typical salesman, that was because he wasn't. He was supposed to come across as your friend or nephew rather than a salesman. The training at Apple, which lasted 40 hours, was by far the highest quality of on-the-job learning that I was exposed to on my journey: It was comprehensive and played to an intelligent audience rather than to the lowest common denominator. Training included four eight-hour shifts wearing white Apple earphones connected to a computer, reading through documents, watching videos, getting pumped up viewing vintage Apple TV ads, and listening to recordings of people from Apple explaining in plain English the ways to operate as a member of the store.

We were told that we were the "first touch point" for customers and that we didn't "have a second chance to make a first impression." We were told that Apple wanted customers to be like "season ticket holders" and that we were recruiters. We were told that our "Genius Bar," where the best-trained among us diagnose problems for customers, brought in many people and that Apple was the "fastest-growing specialty retailer store in history." Our mantra, we were told, was to be "I don't know; let's find out," which meant investigating something together with a customer. (This was also called return to learning, or R2L.) We were not so much told to "be authentic," as employees are told at Starbucks, but were given a more honest variation on this theme: "Be who you are," a recorded voice in training told me. "You know the feeling you get from people who just say what they have to say."

During the first few days, I was trained by a guy named Justin who referenced *The Karate Kid* to describe how the many small things I was learning would soon coalesce into an Apple salesperson version of a wax-on, wax-off karate move. Justin told me that our staff was only 10 percent female and said that *Star Wars* was a common interest among our geeky coworkers. Our work environment was the kind of place where this kind of overheard conversation was not abnormal:

John-Luke, assistant manager: "Hey, I was thinking of you because on the way in to work, I was listening to a radio interview with a philosopher about the self."

Ed, Mac creative and graduate philosophy student: "Do you know—was it an existentialist or Buddhist philosopher being interviewed?"

John-Luke: "I think he was agnostic."

Ed: "Buddhist philosophers are not religious."

John-Luke: "Oh yeah, right."

When we were on break, most of us hung out in the employees-only "back of house." There, employees, most of whom were students or graduate students at nearby San Francisco State, ate lunch, stowed backpacks and messenger bags, used laptops, and talked shop. For most of them, coming into the store was an extension of technology-heavy lives in which Apple products played a large part. Some guys were known as experts on video, others were music freaks, and others were design gurus. The back of house was a clubhouse under assault by the crush of the 40 of us who came and went.

In the back of house, inventory was hung willy-nilly on peg-boards. A microwave oven was wedged precariously on a shelf above two computers that sat on a desk cluttered with paper. Hooks for coats were overloaded with bags and employee clothing. Wire racks were piled high with laptops, returned iPods, and Mac computer towers in for repair. A bulletin board was covered with announcements and snapshots several layers deep. The back of house might have been a mess, but the front of house, the space where customers visited, was an entirely different world. It was designed with care and had its own caretaker, a young man named Marco.

FRONT OF HOUSE

Marco was a tall, well-groomed guy in his mid-twenties. He had short blond hair and typically wore a long-sleeved white or gray shirt under his black Apple T-shirt. Leon intrigued me because of his mastery of the sales floor, but Marco was a character of even more mystique. He was in charge of visuals at the store and was responsible for the layout and upkeep of all the products on display.

Early on, Marco mostly ignored me in the way that a high school senior ignores a freshman—he'd been there long enough to establish his preeminence, and I was a nobody. But one day my training assignment was to shadow him, and as I did so, his facade of icy cool began to break. When I spent an afternoon tagging along, we secured cables and cords to various merchandise with white zip ties, restocked software boxes from the back room, lined up all of the computers and keyboards on nearly invisible lines on the butcher block display tables, and cleaned fingerprint smudges from monitors with baby wipes and spray bottles. Marco told me that everything had to be "symmetrically displayed" and showed me how Apple "vertically merchandises" its products.

Apple's retail division, like the rest of the company, was governed by extremely tight aesthetic guidelines, and Marco was the local design guardian. He moved around the store setting the window design for the month and plugging in new computers—and was capable of a range of duties that nobody else, not even the managers, was capable of. His Lone Wolf McQuade role was enviable because he seemed both indispensable and free to wander around taking care of his self-governed tasks. "At Apple, design supersedes everything, and I mean everything," he said. "There was supposed to be back-to-school stuff in the window starting two weeks ago, but Steve Jobs saw it and did not like it, so he canceled it all at the last minute."

Marco said that someone from corporate could come by the store at any time, and he had to be prepared for such a visit. He was the perfect person to do the job. "What can I say? I've got OCD. I love this stuff," he told me. "At home when I put my TV down on a shelf, I take out my tape measure to make sure it's evenly spaced. I know, I know—I'm nuts."

After the afternoon crush of high school kids, moms pushing baby strollers, and assorted mall shoppers had upset the harmony we had brought to the merchandise, Marco invited me to join forces. "If you can help me out when this place gets tossed up, that would be huge," he said.

The Apple Store sat on the ground level of a mall. When I walked into the large central glass-covered atrium of the mall before a shift, I could smell an odor synthesized from lathers and oils from the Body Shop, ice cream from Häagen-Dazs, fresh buds from a flower store, and Korean barbecue that wafted down from the second-floor food court. The mall was patrolled by security officers dressed to approximate honor guards with broad-brimmed hats. There were unmarked doors and back hallways that we were meant to travel through when carrying inventory.

"Walk around the mall," Leon told me one day. "Look into the other stores and you will see nobody in them. But in here, it's packed." The mall where we worked had many retailers and clothing stores: Victoria's Secret, Banana Republic, Gymboree, Hot Topic, Torrid, and American Eagle Outfitters. There was much activity in the mall but also much boredom. When I walked around on break, other front-line salespeople seemed to be mainly standing around doing nothing: dusting display cabinets, polishing cell phones, and cleaning sunglasses. If Gap was hot in the 1980s and Urban Outfitters in the 1990s, this was the time for the Apple Store chain.

For my first few shifts I was more of an information provider than a seller, and this was clearly what needed to change, because most people asked me questions and left. When I stood at point position in front of the store, I gained a glimpse into how other people in this position—at Wal-Mart and Gap and elsewhere—are most likely bored. Time passed slowly when nobody came in but moved much faster when I was able to engage with a customer. At first most customers had questions that I could not answer, often very basic questions, so I had to find another coworker, such as Leon, who could provide the answer. In doing so, I cut the nascent bonds of trust with my customers. In the few instances when I could actually answer a customer's question, it felt as if I was having a conversation with that customer instead of trying to artificially sell something. When a question arose related to a subject that I had struggled with as a customer, such as finding the best keyboard or buying a hard drive and backup program, I was at ease and felt that I was genuinely helping customers.

I'd had more than seven different Apple computers since the late 1980s, but even though I am a true Apple fan, I did not know much about the full range of products. Once I had completed training and was back in the red zone by myself, without Leon serving as a pair of training wheels, I could see things a bit more clearly. Though it seemed to me that Leon had an easy sale when he was training me, the truth was that his customer, and any of our customers, could (and did) walk out at any minute. I was keenly aware of this as I worked for a few shifts with no computer sales, just bites, and I recognized that there was a big difference between the level of service Leon's customers got from him and what I provided with my limited knowledge at such an early stage.

While I was working at Apple, the company had a good quarter, due in large part to back-to-school sales. Revenue climbed 30 percent to $4.83 billion as the company shipped 8.7 million iPods. The company also sold 1.6 million Macintosh computers. On most days I was lucky to move one or two of these millions of iPods and computers.

On a good day I floated from customer to customer and had very little time to stand around and try to intercept customers on their way in. One day a 30-year-old student from nearby City College asked me which laptop he should purchase. He went back and forth between several options for an hour until I helped him choose one.

At Apple, as elsewhere, sales commissions had been tossed out because they polluted the seller–buyer relationship. But each store and each salesperson had to hit certain targeted "metrics," especially for the "attachments." The store was keen on selling these attachments because they were part of a corporate strategy to connect people to the store on an ongoing basis. From the time I was hired, I was told that if I did not sell these extras, I would see my weekly hours diminish and would not work at ideal times, such as busy weekends and early evenings. In fact, a coworker told me that if he didn't think he would attach anything to a computer sale, he would attempt to palm the customer off on another worker. Typically our morning meetings, in which those assembled went over the day-before sales and attach rates, were pep rallies to pump us up for a day of hitting the right metrics.

One area we couldn't be very familiar with was new products. We were kept in the dark about the new computers and gizmos in the Apple pipeline. My coworkers and I prowled around on Apple rumor websites to glean information, but we were told to not confirm or deny any speculations our customers had. According to training documents, there were three reasons we had to be secretive: Because Apple gets free press by holding back info, because doing so puts competition at a disadvantage, and because it allows Apple to sell through old products.

The culture at Apple was not as forced as at other places because most of us were already part of it long before we started working for the store. Training taught us the basic procedures of store operation and showed us how to sell in a unique way and how to interact with our colleagues, but it pushed the corporate culture less than other companies I had worked for.

One training section called "Fearless Feedback" posed a question: "If the Apple Stores are to achieve the vision of reinventing retail, each person who works in them or supports them must be willing to reinvent themselves. How can we expect our store to be different from any other retailer if we all behave exactly as we did in the places we worked before coming to Apple?" Having moved through five workplaces in two years, I found it an interesting question to think about. My own experience at Apple proved that this was a place where you wanted to change. You got to hang out, share your knowledge, learn, and stay current with cutting-edge technology. I was precariously close to being myself, and customers were sure to pick up on that and respond accordingly. In each discussion with a customer, I continued to feel more at ease, and interactions with my colleagues even came to feel natural. For once, it seemed, all the training documents and associated materials we were given were not so completely bent on shifting people to act in certain ways that they naturally generated cynicism among those forced to change. This training and indoctrination certainly would yield higher sales for the company but it would also teach people to be not only better employees but also somehow better people.

I'd found a place that, while maybe not quite *reinventing* retail, had certainly thought through the pieces enough to find a better approach. Having worked at Apple and seen my own attitude change to fit the culture—having seen me, the nonjoiner, join—I was confident that my journey had come to an appropriate end.

CONCLUSION

SELF-SELECTION

Several months after I left Apple, I went into another Apple Store with a question about a certain type of gift certificate. The cashier, unable to help me, summoned a coworker. This worker, a tall guy with a Brazilian accent, took a glance at the sheet of paper in my hands and adamantly declared that I could purchase something only online and absolutely not in the store. As he explained the store policy to me, I had a feeling that we had met before. It was my old friend Pauliño from Gap, the coworker who had subversively unplugged the scent-emitter that evening long past. Instead of languishing at Gap, he'd made a strong move by jumping to Apple for the Christmas season. There he stood, in front of me, wearing a red Apple T-shirt and a name tag on a lanyard, playing a new role and fighting for his new company. As for me, I had come full circle; I was back to being a customer.

Punching in on the front lines as the critical link between company and customers, each job had required me to take on different responsibilities and roles. By the time I was working that last undercover job as a computer salesman at the Apple Store, I quickly saw how one job experience matched another or was starkly different. Though workplaces changed, systems of dress and conduct remained quite similar. Without fail, in each job I was most drawn to the employee who stood out from the others by having a firm grasp of his or her responsibilities and a heightened level of belief in our particular venture: Big Jim at UPS, Moses at Gap, Zoë and L.J. at Enterprise, Erika at Starbucks, and Leon and Marco at Apple. These were the believers who dominated their retail or service environment and had the most to teach a new recruit like me.

In this futuristic age of computers and wireless communications, it's easy to imagine that the human role in retail and services operations is growing less critical, that companies will soon replace humans with robots on the front lines. But I found that many of the best companies have not only realized that humans matter but have also moved ahead of competitors by finding, hiring, and training great people to work for them. People have become as much of a competitive weapon for many companies as the actual products they sell. Companies succeed by attracting the right potential employees, screening them through online applications and in-person interviews, training them well, and providing a solid culture to join.

In all the jobs I took, I played both the part the company wanted me to play, and the part of the person who would actually be the person to play that part. But as the project progressed, it was harder to separate myself from dual roles as a journalist and an actual employee working a job. Though there was ample time, when folding shirts at Gap or dropping off customers at Enterprise, to wonder about my purpose and size up what, if anything, I was learning, as much as I might have wanted to I couldn't be just a passive observer of the workplaces where I worked.

In an odd way, the various jobs forced me to come to terms with who I am, something that no job-assessment tool could do. I confronted questions I had about conformity by living them out. For whatever reason—whether it is nature or nurture I can't be sure—I am not one overwhelmingly compelled to join up with others. I'm hardwired with whatever it was that kept hunter-gatherers no-madic, not whatever it was that pushed wandering peoples to settle down and eventually raise livestock. My inclinations toward inde-pendent work had been there all along—*needs novelty, a sense of ad-venture, freedom of expression, nonconfining activities*—but I had to live through the experiences to understand that some people have a hard time believing and don't make the best front-line employees.

I never felt at ease in the more constrained environments such as Starbucks, Enterprise, and Gap, where all of our movements were codified, and where the way time was marshaled imposed a form of social control. It was interesting to keep tabs on these workplaces and companies after I had left: In the months following my time at Gap, the CEO was fired by its board of directors. At Starbucks, a surprisingly candid memo from chairman Howard Schultz was leaked and publicized that showed some pronounced cracks in the broad green corporate edifice. In the memo, he worried about the level to which he and his team had overly automated, commod-itized, and sterilized the once theatrical Starbucks experience.

Apple was the rare hourly work environment in which we oper-ated in a looser fashion and were judged by what we did and not so much on what we were doing each minute. But the only company among the many I sampled that had a whiff of the spirit of adven-ture was UPS, a workplace tailored to me in a way none of the other workplaces were. I came to see the other jobs as much less critical; at UPS I gained a strong sense that I was a part of a ticking clock, that I was a part of the thumping, beating heart of capitalism. UPS was the only workplace where I felt as if I was actually learn-ing a craft and helping shape the final product, instead of *acting the part* of a craftsman. UPS was the company that had best married back-end technology with what I came to think of as the company's human front end. On the back end, the computer systems were as high tech as they come, and on the front end you could also argue that the humans were as human as they come. The trip I took to Kansas to ride alongside a couple of drivers validated my feelings about the company and the project—and validated my need to live the brand instead of just reporting on it.

Though I did not understand it at the outset of the project, it made sense by the end that one person could not equally excel at all of the jobs, that someone else might self-select another workplace entirely. Many front-line jobs are ones that job applicants choose by matching themselves up with the company's culture, and those companies that promote this self-selection process are often able to better serve customers. Applicants for the Container Store are fanatical about organization and about sharing their organizational skills with others. People who self-select for UPS are extroverted, athletic, and restless, which are perfect traits for UPS employees but perhaps not so good for Starbucks employees. At UPS, unlike the front-line jobs at other places I worked, employees usually have to work their way up to the front lines by putting in time sorting packages on the overnight shift, as opposed to immediately finding themselves serving customers. (As a seasonal helper, however, I went directly to the front lines.)

To attract employees, you need something to offer them, and that certain something goes under the different names of a brand, a calling, a corporate culture. At its essence, this force is larger than a person; it is a force that feels worth allying with and merging into. Some companies shape whatever their cultural needs are to the population that they hope to recruit and employ. In the best situations, the applicant hears a calling to the company long before applying; there is something out there that makes the place seem like the right fit. When working at that place, there is a moment when you feel alive, when you are no longer questioning and thinking about life on the outside, life before the job, and life after the job— when you are the job. For some it is being absorbed in the moment, frenetically pumping out espresso beverages; for me it was at the end of a long, hard day at UPS delivering packages. Part of what I learned by the end of the experiment was that there was a deeper subtext to UPS founder James Casey's phrase, that *anybody* could deliver packages. There was more to it than just good training; a company actually had to expend some effort in finding the right person. The truth was that anybody *could* deliver the packages, but it was better if you found somebody who actually *wanted* to deliver the packages.

ON DECEMBER 23, when Carolyn and I drove past the Christmas tree lot we passed every morning at around 10:40, the only trees left were runts—the leftover two- and three-foot trees that few people bother with. Though UPS in December is associated in many people's minds with Christmas, it was in fact pretty far from our minds. "Oh, you're an elf," one of my friends said when I described my job. On the truck, with no radio, I had been spared the litany of Christmas songs and the packed stores, even as much as I had been in the thick of it. I did, however, hear an awe-inspiring Bing Crosby rendition of "White Christmas" on the radio while driving to work one day. It sounded genuine and sweet and timeless and made the season feel important and not crass and commercial. As Christmas got closer, I observed a spike in hand-wrapped gifts sent from parents to kids. A couple of recipients made note of this. "Cookies from my mom," they told me. *Pause*. "She bakes them for me every Christmas."

In my mind right then, we were part of a higher calling—connecting people with love, desire, loss, friendship, and family. If your job was to deliver all year, then the act of delivering Christmas presents pretty much epitomized the idea that by creating real meaning for customers, people would find meaning in their jobs.

Those last days before Christmas, it was all Amazon, all the time. The home scenes I traveled through blurred into one—delivering a bottle of Rémy Martin to a Polish immigrant family hunkered down in the kitchen cooking, climbing over fresh cement to put down packages by a red front door, sharing a cupcake with an elderly woman. True, by the end of each day, all I wanted to do was throw packages out of the truck at their target addresses. But teamwork and some sort of moral imperative to stay on task kept me at it. Working long days and some overtime, I was walking away with around $85 a day. I was worn down, focused solely on crossing the finish line that was Christmas Eve.

As I walked into the building the final morning of the holiday rush—December 24—there was a definite hush and a slowing of motion, a disquieting calm that had come over the building. I saw one of the graveyard shift preloaders with his backpack on, headed for the door, a signal that he was already done. The center had met its milestone of Christmas Eve day and, for the first time since I'd been there, the unrelenting flow of goods had come to a halt.

It felt great to make it to that last day. Everyone massed for a meeting, and there was a big raffle of goods. I scored a cool black UPS logo hat. A driver named Ronald went to claim his prize and saluted management, saying that in the 12 years working at UPS he had never seen a Christmas season run so smoothly.

It was a day of big rains, but Carolyn and I had only one Christmas crisis; a woman told me that Amazon had sent her daughter the wrong package and that another kid in a nearby city had received her present. This was, unfortunately, not something we could really help out with. We suggested she get in touch with Amazon. I delivered a parcel to one guy who confided in me that he would have been "up the creek" had I not arrived.

On the way back to the building, Carolyn offered me her UPS-issue holiday turkey because her UPS-driver husband had also received one. She said it was a "step above a Butterball." The Christmas in store for me would involve a lot of sleep, not cooking a bird, but I was tempted.

There I had been, just three weeks before, sitting at my desk distracted by email and reading books and magazine articles about branding and corporate culture. Then, sporting brown from head to toe, I physically moved packages to the people of San Francisco. With no great perceived effort on its part, UPS had inculcated me. I had delivered several thousand packages and I had felt what it was like to represent UPS, to *be* UPS. I went in thinking that I'd be working at another soulless company, but I was wrong. I thought it would be a cold, sterile work environment, yet it was vibrant. People were not automatons; they were living in the moment. The heightened package volume certainly helped foster this feeling that war correspondents describe as being alive and aware of every waking second. As an employee I got a chance to see what my career trajectory might look like. I went from thinking it would be a fun experiment to maybe wanting to stay longer. Wearing a uniform and learning the on-the-job lingo pulled me in and made me feel like a part of the group. Then the hard physical work drained me and I wanted to flee. Then I got interested in staying and doing a good job. Other drivers welcomed me and shared with me their own ways in. I went in neutral and came out a believer. I went in as an anybody, and I came out as a somebody.

Finally, as Carolyn and I pulled into the building, it was the end of the day on December 24. The fourth-floor space was almost filled with trucks, so many that there was little room to park, and the trucks were squeezed in like a three-dimensional brown metal jigsaw puzzle. I shook hands with Carolyn as she thanked me for all of my work, though it felt like a hug would have been more in order. She gave me an envelope with a $20 bill and a Christmas card that read "Thank you, thank you, thank you. I could not have done it without you. I hope you get the job of your dreams. Happy holidays, Carolyn."

After a Christmas spent taking it easy and resting before the new year, I went back the first week of January to return my uniform and collect my last paycheck. Jed Barnes from HR was there to check off names, hand out envelopes, and give a firm handshake and thanks. There was a sign-up form for those of us who wanted to be called in to work the preload. I was tempted to sign up, to keep my investment in the company growing and to stay a part of it. I managed to keep the few pieces of my uniform that Carolyn had given me, and a year later I'd pull on the warm brown quilted vest and feel a sense of power and place.

Several months after Christmas, I had to send some paperwork to my accountant by overnight delivery. Once the package had been sent, via UPS, I realized that I did not write down the suite number in his office building. I felt a quick surge of concern until I thought about how it all worked. The package would come off the belt and be put on the truck, the driver would pull it out on the loading dock in the high-rise building in downtown Oakland. He'd see there was no suite number, and he'd ask around or, more likely, he'd know Chas and that his office was on the ninth floor. He would, like so many UPS drivers, serve as that critical human link. Sure enough, a cell phone call came through the next day directly from the driver. He just wanted to confirm that suite 900 was the right place. We were in good shape. And the connection was still there. *I'm one of you*, I wanted to tell him.

ENDNOTES

INTRODUCTION: BECOMING ONE OF THEM

page 5: "knowledge worker" from Peter Drucker, *Post-Capitalist Society* (New York: HarperBusiness, 1993), 8.

page 8: "Anybody can deliver packages" from Philip Hamburger, "Ah Packages!" *The New Yorker*, May 10, 1947.

CHAPTER 1. THE OTHER ARMY

page 22: "experienced drivers vividly recall" from Robert Putnam, *Better Together* (New York: Simon & Schuster, 2003), 211.

page 28: "represents membership in a collective enterprise" from Putnam, *Better Together*, 212.

page 35: Tom Watson Jr. speech cited in John P. Kotter and James L. Heskett, *Corporate Culture and Performance* (New York: Free Press, 1992), 17.

page 35: "physical environment, language, technology," etc., from Edgar Schein, *Organizational Culture and Leadership*, 2nd ed. (San Francisco: Jossey-Bass, 1992), 17.

page 37: "The more efficient they are" from Deborah Orr, "Delivering America," *Forbes*, October 4, 2004.

page 38: "aspects of the company parallel military behaviors" from Putnam, *Better Together*, 206.

page 44: C. L. Kane, *The Tightest Ship: UPS Exposé* (Cogan Station, PA: self-published, 1995), 48, 119, 66.

Additional material about Worldport came from John McPhee, "Annals of Transport: Out in the Sort," *The New Yorker*, April 18, 2005.

CHAPTER 2. ONE GREAT EMPLOYEE

page 51: "non-farm payrolls," from *Wall Street Journal*, June 3, 2005.

page 52: "service workers" from Peter Drucker, *Post-Capitalist Society* (New York: HarperBusiness, 1993), 8.

page 70: "Woodworth Personal Data Sheet," from Margaret Talbot, "The Rorschach Chronicles," *New York Times Magazine*, October 17, 1999.

page 71: Background on Dr. David Scarborough and his work from David Scarborough and Mark John Somers, *Neural Networks in Organizational Research* (Washington, D.C.: American Psychological Association, 2006).

CHAPTER 3. TWO TRUTHS AND ONE LIE

page 113: "Smash Mouth," from Jordan Harper, "Smashed Mouth?" *Riverfront Times*, June 2, 2004.

CHAPTER 4. INTO THE FOLD

page 119: "We're passionate that you be you," from *Welcome to Gap Inc.*, 2005, 28.

page 126: Slavomir Rawicz, *The Long Walk* (North Salem, NY: Adventure Library, 1999).

page 127: "Much of what is at the heart of a culture," from Edgar Schein, *Organizational Culture and Leadership*, 2nd ed. (San Francisco: Jossey-Bass, 1992), 13.

page 134: Background on Gap style and inventiveness: Paul Goldberger, "The Sameness of Things," *New York Times Magazine*, April 6, 1997.

page 134: "Without a defining product," from Julia Boorstin, "Fashion Victim," *Forbes*, April 17, 2006.

page 134: "According to retail experts," from Paco Underhill, *Why We Buy* (New York: Simon & Schuster, 2000), 184.

page 136: Background on Robert Boleyn and Gap lawsuit from Jenny Strasburg, "Uniform Resistance," *San Francisco Chronicle*, February 5, 2003.

page 138: Alvin Collis interview, October 24, 2006.

page 138: Jeff Daniel interview, May 10, 2006.

CHAPTER 5. GET BIG, STAY SMALL

page 156: "core settings of informal public life," from Ray Oldenburg, *The Great Good Place* (New York: Marlowe, 1997), 15.

page 156: "Where once there were places," from Oldenburg, *The Great Good Place*, 205.

page 156: "there is no neutral ground," from Oldenburg, *The Great Good Place*, 22.

page 157: "not yet the ideal Third Place," from Howard Schultz and Dori Jones Yang, *Pour Your Heart into It* (New York: Hyperion, 1997), 120.

page 157: "The nonplace that takes over," from Oldenburg, *The Great Good Place*, 205.

page 164: "distracted by our size," from Schultz, *Pour Your Heart into It*, 259.

page 166: "as the accumulated shared learning," from Schein, *Organizational Culture and Leadership*, 2nd ed., 10.

page 167: "common or pervasive ways of acting," from Kotter and Heskett, *Corporate Culture and Performance*, 5.

page 182: "Like climbing a big mountain," from Jim Collins and Jerry Porras, *Built to Last* (New York: HarperBusiness, 1994), 8.

CHAPTER 6. IN THE RED ZONE

No sources.

CONCLUSION: SELF-SELECTION

No sources.

ACKNOWLEDGMENTS

Green Apron Awards for all: I chiefly owe my words of thanks to all of the partners, coworkers, assistant managers, management trainees, area managers, Mac specialists, geniuses, creatives, drivers, loaders, shift supervisors, managers, coaches, buddies, and baristas who unknowingly let me into their midst and were patient enough to teach me their crafts while serving as unwitting subjects for this book. Thanks also to Dan McMackin, Marc Giuffre, Carol Rea, April Nelson, and Lon Wallis of UPS. Thanks to Elizabeth Gould, Michael Megalli, Glasgow Phillips, Tucker Nichols, John Maybury, Lisa Hamilton, and Emily McManus for reviewing this book in manuscript form and both tightening the prose and asking for clarification. Additional thanks to Tucker Nichols for being the kind of sounding board one needs when occasionally lost in the retail wilderness. Thanks to Joel Swerdlow and Simon Frankel for advice en route, to Clay Walker and Aaron Gigliotti, to photographer Sven Wiederholt, to Cary Zips for running the Canadian operations, to Michelle Jeffers in the research department, and to my team at Ground Level Research. Thanks to my parents Chuck and Diane Frankel. Thanks to Bert Phillips and Happy Fowler in Colorado, and Aaron Cooperman at Sol Mountain Touring in British Columbia for high-altitude room and board, and to Eddy Peterson for a low-altitude apartment in New York City. Thanks to Satoko Furuta for many late-night dinners, much patience, and making life together sweet. Thanks to my agent Bonnie Nadell and to Marion Maneker at Collins for giving the green light to this project. Thanks to Angie Lee, Ben Loehnen, Teresa Brady, and Sarah Brown at Collins. Finally, thanks to my editor, Genoveva Llosa, for thoughtfully and enthusiastically shaping this book into its final form.

INDEX

Abercrombie & Fitch, 139
accidents and injuries, 23, 26
advertising:
  Apple Store, 192
  Gap, 135, 145
  UPS, 12
Airborne, 29, 30
airplanes, 81–82
  UPS, 45–47
Amazon.com, 32, 206
American Eagle Outfitters, 196
Applebee's, 88
Apple Store, 187–99, 201, 202, 203
  advertising, 192
  application and interview, 191–92
  corporate culture, 187–99
  customers, 189–90, 192–94, 196–99
  dress code, 187–88, 194, 201

  employees, 187–99
  management, 190, 191, 192
  metrics, 197–98
  store design, 194–96
  training, 187–90, 192–94, 198–99
applications and interviews, 51–78, 202
  Apple Store, 191–92
  Container Store, 53–58, 74–78
  Enterprise Rent-A-Car, 80–85
  Gap, 120
  Home Depot, 58–62, 64
  online, 58–67, 72–74, 78, 82–83, 191, 202
  psychological tests, 68–78
  Starbucks, 151, 183–84
  UPS, 11–13
  Whole Foods, 62–67
Apprentice, The (TV show), 97
Avis, 87, 100

Banana Republic, 121, 196
Barnes, Jed, 11, 13, 208
Bass, 29
Bean, L.L., 29, 32
Best Buy, 67, 71, 72
BHAG, 181–82
Birkman, Roger W., 68
Birkman test, 68–69
body language, 120
Body Shop, 195
Boleyn, Robert, 136
Boone, Garrett, 57
Borders, 139
boredom, 124, 128, 146, 147, 196
branding, 87–88, 158
Budget, 100, 113
bullying technique, 102–103

Canada, 81
Carhartt, 29
Casey, James, 8, 44, 205
catalogs, 53–54
Chevrolet, 106, 107
Chicago, 45
Chico's, 136
Christmas, 15, 25–27, 32, 38, 41, 120, 205–208
Chrysler, 105
Collins, Jim, 181
Collis, Alvin, 138
computers, 40, 187, 202
    Apple Store, 187–99

Enterprise Rent-A-Car, 79, 99–100
online applications, 58–67, 72–74, 78, 82–83, 191, 202
Starbucks, 152
UPS, 42, 43, 48, 203
consumerism, 8
Container Store, 5, 53–58, 74–78, 80, 204
    application and interview, 53–58, 74–78
    corporate culture, 55–58, 74–78
    employees, 53, 54–58, 76–77
    salaries, 57
corporate culture, 4–6, 29, 35–36, 166–67, 202, 204
    Apple Store, 187–99
    Container Store, 55–58, 74–78
    Enterprise Rent-A-Car, 79–117
    Gap, 119–47
    Starbucks, 149–86
    UPS, 4, 11–49
    Whole Foods, 62–67
Costco, 54
Cotter, John, 167
Crate & Barrel, 32
Curves, 174
customers, 201
    Apple Store, 189–90, 192–94, 196–99

Enterprise Rent-A-Car, 89–91, 98, 101–113

Gap, 120, 124, 125, 129, 131, 132, 140, 143–46

Starbucks, 152–56, 158–59, 177, 179, 181–84

UPS, 13, 15–16, 18, 33, 36–37, 206

customer service, 67, 73, 89, 90, 123, 143–44, 159

Dallas, 57

Daniel, Jeff, 138–39

data, employee, 68–74

Davis, Ben, 29

delivery information acquisition device (DIAD), 13, 14, 16, 18–19, 20, 21, 34

Dell computers, 32

"Denver concept," 134

design, store, 35, 134, 151, 184, 194–95

Detroit, 45

DHL, 37

Dickies, 29

dress code, 36, 87, 95, 136–37

Apple Store, 187–88, 194, 201

Enterprise Rent-A-Car, 87, 96–97, 98

Gap, 119, 125, 135–37

Starbucks, 161, 174

vs. uniforms, 136–37

UPS, 4, 12, 15, 16, 17, 18, 20, 26, 27–30

Drexler, Mickey, 134

Drucker, Peter, 52

DVDs, company, 57–58, 122, 123, 141, 142, 173–74, 175

eBay, 29

Eisler, Staci, 160–61

employees, 6, 7, 204

Apple Store, 187–99

Container Store, 53, 54–58, 76–77

Enterprise Rent-A-Car, 79–117

Gap, 119–47

Starbucks, 149–86

UPS, 11–49, 203–208

Whole Foods, 62, 63, 64

Enterprise Rent-A-Car, 78, 79–117, 150, 202, 203

application and interview, 80–85

branches, 98–109

corporate culture, 79–117

customers, 89–91, 98, 101–113

dissatisfaction, 114–17

employees, 79–117

insurance products, 89–91, 102–104

management, 82, 85, 87, 99, 113, 114

Enterprise Rent-A-Car (*cont.*)
 phone shopping, 100–101
 salary, 84, 92, 94
 technology, 79, 99–100
 training and orientation,
  79–81, 86–98
Enterprise Service Quality
 Index (ESQi), 111–13
European customers, 132, 144
Exceeding Expectations, 84

FailingEnterprise.com, 114–17
Farmer, Fanny, 32
Faubert, Ed, 171
favorable self-presentation, 71–72
FedEx, 12, 29, 37
Fisher, Don, 121
Fisher, Doris, 121
flagship store, 131
Florida, 113
Forbes, 37
Forth & Towne, 121
Fortune, 52, 57

Gap, 7, 77, 119–47, 150, 192,
  196, 201, 202, 203
 advertising, 135, 145
 application and interview, 120
 corporate culture, 119–47
 credit cards, 143–46
 customers, 120, 124, 125, 129,
  131, 132, 140, 143–46

denim department, 128–35
dress code, 119, 125, 135–37
employees, 119–47
fitting rooms, 124, 125
folding clothes, 122, 124, 125,
 128, 147
management, 122, 123, 130,
 141–43
music, 137–39
salary, 143
slumping sales, 133–34, 146
store design, 134
training, 119, 122, 129–36
GM, 106
Graco, 32
Green Apron Book, 164–67
Gymboree, 196

Häagen-Dazs, 195
H&M, 146
harassment, 111
Hassi, Eileen, 161–62, 164
health insurance, 52, 94, 166
Hertz, 87, 100
Heskett, James, 167
hiring, 51–78, 202
 Apple Store, 191–92
 Container Store, 53–58, 74–78
 Enterprise Rent-A-Car, 80–85
 Gap, 120
 Home Depot, 58–62, 64
 psychological tests, 68–78

Starbucks, 151, 183–84
UPS, 11–13
Whole Foods, 62–67
See also applications and inter-
　views
holiday season, 15, 16, 21, 25–
　27, 38, 41, 120, 128, 205–208
Home Depot, 5, 51, 58–62, 67,
　80, 192
　application and interview,
　58–62, 64
Hot Topic, 196
HSN, 32
Hummer, 106, 107

IBM, 35
individuality, 67, 74, 203
insurance, 99
　car, 89–91, 102–104
　health, 52, 94, 166
International Coffee Organiza-
　tion, 157
interviews. *See* applications and
　interviews
Iraq war, 43

Jay-Z, 137
Jeep, 105
Jobs, Steve, 192, 195

Kane, Charlie, *The Tightest
　Ship: UPS Exposé,* 44

Kansas, UPS operations in,
　42–43
kindergarten cultural arche-
　type, 167, 171
Kitchin, Patrick, 136

labor unions, 32
Lands' End, 32
Learning Journey Guide, 152
Levi's, 121, 126, 131
Loss Prevention (LP), 140–41

management, 69, 203
　Apple Store, 190, 191, 192
　Enterprise Rent-A-Car, 82, 85,
　　87, 99, 113, 114
　Gap, 122, 123, 130, 141–43
　Starbucks, 149, 155, 161–62,
　　165–67, 168–73, 185
　UPS, 14, 25, 26, 31, 38, 44
Mercedes, 105
Mexico, 33
military, 7, 38, 43, 44, 70
mini-relationships, 144
Minnesota Multiphasic Person-
　ality Inventory, 70
Mitsubishi, 105
Mullen, John, 57
music, 137–39
　Gap, 137–39
　Starbucks, 137–39, 176–77
Muzak, 137–38

New York City, 65, 66, 67
nonsmart labels, 48
NORs, 140

OfficeMax, 97
Oldenburg, Ray, 156, 157
Old Navy, 121
Omaha Steaks, 32
online applications, 58–67, 72–
    74, 78, 82–83, 191, 202
overtime, 41, 84

payroll, 73
Penney, JC, 133
physical environment, design
    of, 35, 134, 151, 184, 194–95
Piperlime, 121
Polo Ralph Lauren, 136
Pottery Barn, 32
Pressler, Paul, 121, 134, 142
psychological tests, 68–78
Putnam, Robert, 28, 38

QVC, 32

Real Simple, 66
Red Bull, 93
REI, 53
religion, 90–91, 193
retail industry, 6, 7, 19, 23, 52,
    56, 126, 134, 138, 188, 202.
    See also specific companies

Ritual Coffee Roasters, 162–64
Rock River Music, 138
role-playing, 89

salaries, 51–52
  Container Store, 57
  Enterprise Rent-A-Car, 84, 92,
    94
  Gap, 143
  UPS, 12, 41
San Francisco, 4, 15, 23, 24–25,
    32, 53, 63, 65, 79, 109, 121
  Apple Store operations, 191–99
  Enterprise Rent-A-Car opera-
    tions, 79–117
  Starbucks operations, 151–86
  UPS operations, 15–42, 207
Sanka, 162
Scarborough, David, 71, 73–74
Schein, Edgar, 127, 166
Schultz, Howard, 150, 156–57,
    164, 203
Seattle, 162, 164, 183
See's Candies, 32
Sephora, 139
shoplifting, 141
sick days, 38
Skandia shelving, 57
smart labels, 48
Starbucks, 5, 7, 9, 51, 138,
    149–86, 188, 192, 193, 202,
    203, 204

applications, 151, 183–84

corporate culture, 149–86

customers, 152–56, 158–59, 177, 179, 181–84

deployment maps, 179

dress code, 161, 174

efficiency system failures, 179–81

employees, 149–86

Experience Workshop, 173–76

Green Apron Book, 164–67

growth of, 157, 164

jargon, 153–54

locations, 159–61, 164

making drinks, 171–73, 177

management, 149, 155, 161–62, 165–67, 168–73, 185

music, 138–39, 176–77

sizing system, 153–54, 172, 182, 184

Snapshots, 181–83

store design, 151, 184

technology, 152

as third place, 156–59

tips, 178–79

training, 152–56, 164–76, 183–84

turnover, 183

Stiefel, Barry, 114, 115

surveillance, 140–41

Taylor, Frederick Winslow, 6

Taylor, Jack, 80, 110

Teamsters, 32

technology, 36, 202

Apple, 187–99

Enterprise Rent-A-Car, 79, 99–100

Starbucks, 152

UPS, 18–19, 24, 34, 40, 42–49, 203

temp workers, 51

tests, psychological, 68–78

Texas, 57, 62

theft, 141

Thematic Apperception Test, 70

third places, 156–59

Tindell, Kip, 57

Tooker, Jeremy, 162

Torrefazione Italia, 161–62

Torrid, 196

Toyota, 106

training, 167

Apple Store, 187–90, 192–94, 198–99

Enterprise Rent-A-Car, 79–81, 86–98

Gap, 119, 122, 129–36

Starbucks, 152–56, 164–76, 183–84

UPS, 13–15

Trump, Donald, 97

turnover, employee, 7, 56, 72, 73, 104, 146, 167, 183

Underhill, Paco, *Why We Buy,* 126

Unicro-style tests, 71–74

uniforms, 29–30

  dress codes vs., 136–37

  UPS, 4, 12, 15, 16, 17, 18, 20, 26, 27–30

U.S. Postal Service, 37

unit load devices (ULDs), 44–45

UPS, 2, 3–4, 8–9, 11–49, 104, 107, 202, 203–208

  accidents and injuries, 23, 26

  advertising, 12

  airplanes, 45–47

  application and interview, 11–13

  corporate culture, 4, 11–49

  customers, 13, 15–16, 18, 33, 36–37, 206

  deliveryman stereotype, 15, 18, 20, 24–25, 44

  delivery system, 15–16, 21, 25–27, 33, 37–49

  employees, 15–49, 203–208

  hiring, 11–13

  holiday season, 15, 16, 21, 25–27, 38, 41, 205–208

  management, 14, 25, 26, 31, 38, 44

  orientation and training, 13–15

  salary, 12, 41

  teamwork, 32–42

  technology, 18–19, 24, 34, 40, 42–49, 203

  uniform, 4, 12, 15, 16, 17, 18, 20, 26, 27–30

  Worldport Facility, 39, 42–49

Urban Outfitters, 196

Vancouver, 81, 172

Victoria's Secret, 196

VW, 107

wages. *See* salaries

Wall Street Journal, 51, 142

Wal-Mart, 32, 121, 196

Watson, Tom, Jr., 35

weather, 20

Whole Foods, 56, 62–67, 71, 72, 80

  application and interview, 62–67

  corporate culture, 62–67

Woodworth Personal Data Sheet, 70

Workforce Management, 52

ALEX FRANKEL has reported on business culture for *Wired*, *The New York Times Magazine*, *Outside*, and other publications. He is also the author of *Wordcraft: The Art of Turning Little Words into Big Business*. He lives in San Francisco.